AUD

by
F.G. RAYER, T.Eng.(CEI), Assoc. IERE

BERNARD BABANI (publishing) LTD
THE GRAMPIANS
SHEPHERDS BUSH ROAD
LONDON W6 7NF
ENGLAND

PLEASE NOTE

© 1981 BERNARD BABANI (publishing) LTD

First Published — July 1981
Reprinted — July 1988
Reprinted — May 1991

British Library Cataloguing in Publication Data
Rayer, F.G.
    Audio projects
    1. High-fidelity sound systems — Amateurs' manuals
    I. Title
    621.389'3   TK7881.7

    ISBN 0 85934 065 1

Printed and bound in Great Britain by Cox & Wyman, Reading

CONTENTS

MISCELLANEOUS PROJECTS

INTRODUCTION

Note on Components

Resistors can all be ¼ watt, unless otherwise noted. The actual power dissipated in many circuit positions is much less than this, but such resistors are readily obtainable. Thus ¼w 5 per-cent resistors can be fitted throughout with very few exceptions.

With potentiometers, values such as 22k and 25k are interchangeable, as are 250k and 220k, or 470k and 500k or 0.5 megohm. Potentiometers are usually small carbon types. They are made in linear, semi-log, log and anti-log types. These terms refer to the amount of resistance change encountered for a given rotation of the control spindle or control knob. Circuits will operate with any type, but awkward crowding of adjustment can be expected with substitutions of this nature. For gain or volume control, logarithmic controls are usual.

Capacitors for audio circuits can be polyester, polystyrene, paper, polycarbonate, or electrolytic. Silvered mica are suitable but seldom used because of cost. For general audio use, there is considerable latitude in capacitors.

There is also usually latitude in electrolytic capacitor values. For by-pass purposes, 100 μF or 120 μF or 125 μF are interchangeable, as are 200 μF, 220 μF or 250 μF. Similar considerations apply to other values, including those of about 1 μF to 10 μF for inter-stage coupling, where near values can be used.

All capacitors should have a voltage rating at least equal to the voltage present across them. This may govern the selection. As example, if an amplifier is to run from 9v, 10v capacitors can be used. But these would be inadequate if a higher voltage were to be adopted. It might then be necessary to fit 16v, 25v or other ratings. These could be used with the 9v supply, but would generally not be fitted if only 9v would be employed, for economy.

Most small value non-polarised capacitors will easily have a high enough voltage rating, as this will probably be 100v or more. But with disc ceramic, electrolytics and tantalum bead capacitors, the rating may be 3v, 6.3v or otherwise inadequate for some circuit position, so it should always be checked.

Various knobs, dials, scales and cases allow attractive pieces of equipment to be made. Jacks and sockets are dealt with elsewhere, and should allow easy interconnecting of all units.

In many circuits different transistors or ICs can be used, with appropriate changes to suit.

Power Supplies

It is generally convenient to incorporate the power supply for AC mains operation in the equipment. The circuit at A in Figure 1 is extensively used, with transformer, rectifiers, and capacitor C1 to suit the current load and voltage required.

Mains transformer T1 may have a tapped primary, for 200v, 220v, 240v or other range of inputs. Some transformers have windings which may be placed in parallel for 120v, or series for 240v. In each case phase of connection must be correct.

The voltage arising across capacitor C1, with no load, will be approximately 1.4 times the RMS rating of the transformer

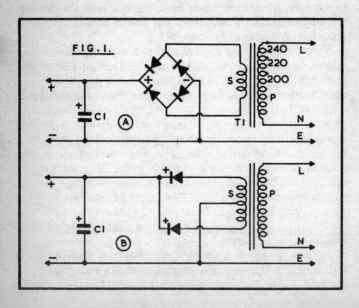

secondary S. The voltage drops when current is drawn. The severity of this drop depends on the resistance of secondary S (and primary P) and with syllabic rate loads, the capacitance of C1. The rectifiers also contribute to the drop, but this is small with silicon diodes.

Some typical characteristics of power supply units are as follows:

3 Watt amplifier, drain 25mA to 200mA. Secondary S, 17v 500mA. C1 1250 μF 25v. Approximate output, 22v.

10 Watt amplifier, drain 50mA to 800mA. Secondary S 18v 1.5A. C1 4500 μF 25v. Approximate output 24v.

Amplifiers will have a particular maximum supply voltage, which must not be exceeded. Voltage will be at maximum when the amplifier is drawing least current. If the voltage is then too high, steps must be taken to reduce it. A lower voltage secondary (or lower voltage tap if available) would be preferred. If this is not available, and the PSU can easily supply more than adequate current, and voltage is only a little too high with the amplifier drawing minimum current, then a resistor may be placed across C1. This imposes an additional steady load. A small drop in secondary voltage can be obtained by using the highest primary tapping — e.g., that for 250v input, even if the mains are 240v or less.

Where maximum possible output will not be wanted from an amplifier the situation is not likely to present difficult. Secondary S can be of slightly lower voltage rating, so that even with minimum load the voltage at C1 is below the maximum rating for the amplifier.

For home-built amplifiers, a transformer with multi-tapped secondary is very useful. This may have tappings at 0, 12, 15, 20, 24 and 30v. Other voltages can be obtained by choice of taps. As example, 12v and 30v taps for 18v, or 20v and 30v taps for 10v. In this way a wide range of equipment can be catered for, and an amplifier can be tested initially on reduced voltage.

1N4002 or similar rectifiers are convenient for up to 1A, with similar 2A or other appropriate rectifiers for greater loads. A fuse may be placed in one secondary lead.

Circuit B is less often used, and requires a centre-tapped secondary. The overall voltage of the secondary here is twice that of A. Thus if A employed a 15v secondary, B would use a 15–0–15V secondary, or 30v winding with centre-tap. B lends itself much less readily to voltage adjustment by means of a tapped secondary.

Separate PSU

Figure 2 shows layout of a power supply unit which can be used for amplifiers (or other equipment). Mains conductors are anchored at a tagstrip, and the on-off switch is placed on the case front. The primary P is for 240v, or as required.

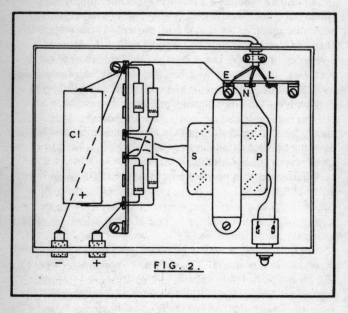

FIG. 2.

Four silicon diodes and the smoothing capacitor are mounted on a second tagstrip. A band indicates diode positive. The transformer secondary voltage will depend on the output wanted, as explained. A tapped transformer will permit the same PSU being used for a range of output voltages. Diodes of 1A rating, 50 or 100 PIV, will be suitable for currents of up to 1 ampere, and 2A or 3A diodes are fitted where these larger currents are required. The current rating of the transformer secondary is similarly arranged to suit the maximum load which will be applied.

Capacitor C1 needs to be of large value (generally some thousands of microfarads) and may be a high-ripple component, with a voltage rating of about 1.5 times that of the transformer secondary. Sockets take plugs for external leads from the unit. In most amplifiers, additional smoothing will be present in the amplifier itself, for early stages.

A PSU of this type is not regulated, and its voltage depends somewhat on load. However, most popular audio amplifier circuits are designed to operate from this type of circuit, which has the advantage of requiring few components.

Actual construction of the PSU section should be with safety in mind. Draw current from a plug with 2A fuse, or have a low-rating fuse in the Live circuit at T1. Primary connecting points should be so arranged that they cannot be touched when handling the equipment normally, out of its case. A single-pole on-off switch should be placed in the Live side of the circuit (not Neutral).

No shock dangers are normally associated with the secondary or output side of a transformer coupled PSU of this type. However, some large amplifiers employ 30v or more, and in certain circumstances some shock hazard may be associated with these voltages.

Battery Running

Dry battery working is satisfactory for small amplifiers. These often use a 9v or 12v supply. It may be from 6 x 1.5v cells for 9v, or 8 x 1.5v cells for 12v. Large dry cells have enough capacity for intermittent use with moderately high power, as in a loud hailer. An increase in voltage should not be made unless it has been checked that the integrated circuit, transistors, or operating conditions generally permit this.

Larger power portable equipment for continuous use can operate from a 12v or 24v accumulator supply, or from other rechargeable cells. Equipment for 12v is convenient where a vehicle supply will be available.

PRE-AMPLIFIERS AND MIXERS

1-Stage Preamplifier

Where volume is insufficient due to the input to the main
amplifier being too low, a preamplifier stage can be added to
correct this. Such a preamplifier is often included in a tone
control unit, to compensate for losses in the latter. Or it may
be present in the main amplifier. Sometimes alternative inputs
will be available, so that the preamplifier can be placed in
circuit or excluded, as necessary.

Figure 3 is a basic preamplifier which can be adapted for
many purposes. When the 2-way switch is at A—A, inputs are
amplified. When this switch is at B—B, operation is straight
through without amplification.

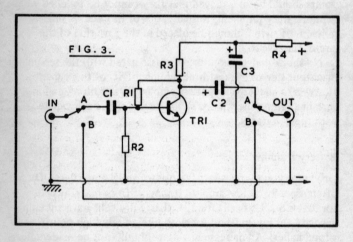

C1 is for base coupling and provides DC isolation from
external circuits. C2 is the output coupling capacitor. In some
circuits it can be omitted, as it will already be present in the
following main amplifier, or tone control input circuit. If the
preamplifier is going to be used with various external units, C2
should be included.

A 12v to 15v supply for this stage is convenient, but

anything from 9v upwards can be used. Where the supply line exceeds about 15v, R4 can be increased in value so that a high-resistance voltmeter across C3 shows about 12v. Alternatively, measure the stage current and calculate R4 from Ohm's Law, which is more accurate.

R1 and R2 set the base conditions relative to collector voltage, which depends on R3 and the line voltage. With a low noise transistor and low collector current, very good results can be obtained. It is possible to reduce R3 to 15k or 10k, and reduce R1 to 1 megohm for operation at a slightly higher current level.

For adjustment of performance, with alternative transistors, only one resistor need be modified. This may be R1. See below

Components for 1-Stage Preamplifier, Figure 3

R1	1.8 megohm	R2	270k
R3	47k	R4	8.2k
C1	0.1 μF	C2	2 μF
Tr1	BC109	C3	220 μF 15v
2-pole 2-way switch		Sockets, board, etc.	

Low-level Class A Stages

In Figure 3 stabilisation of working is obtained by R2, and by supplying base current through R1 which is taken to the collector, and whose upper potential depends on the voltage drop in R3, which in turn depends on collector current. In such circumstances, satisfactory results are obtained with a wide spread in transistors, resistor values, and line voltages.

Alternative transistors, capable of satisfactory results, may need larger base and collector currents. In some circuits, R2 will be omitted, reliance being placed on supplying R1 through R3 to achieve stability, or upon base current being limited by the large value at R1.

If a preamplifier of this kind does not provide the gain expected, or is very readily overloaded, this is easily corrected so that the particular transistor used can operate satisfactorily.

Base current can be increased by increasing the value of R2, or by omitting R2, or by reducing the value of R1. Both base and collector currents increase, when R3 is reduced in value. This relationship between collector current and base current of

any transistor depends on its current gain, which can range
from 50 or less to several hundred, for various types generally
used as small audio amplifiers.

With a meter connected between R3 and the positive line,
to show current drawn, suitable potentiometers may be
substituted for R1 and R3. These may have fixed resistors in
series with them, to avoid possible damage with careless setting.
R1 could be substituted by a 2 megohm control with 100k
resistor in series, and R3 by a 50k potentiometer with 4.7k
series resistor. Results, and current drawn, can then be
checked over a wide range of conditions, and the nearest
appropriate fixed value resistors can be inserted afterwards.

A 30dB Preamplifier

This 2-stage preamplifier has an overall gain of approximately
30dB, and is directly coupled so that it provides a wide
frequency response. Input has DC isolation by C1, and output
is isolated by C3, Figure 4.

The negative feedback provides DC stabilisation for the two

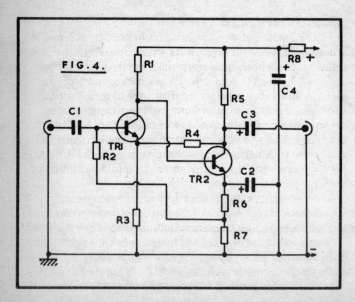

FIG.4.

8

amplifiers. Tr1 base potential is derived from the divider R6/R7, so depends on Tr2 emitter current, and changes in Tr1 collector current alter the voltage drop across R1, and thus the base potential of Tr2. Changes in Tr2 collector voltage, due to the current passing through R5, similarly help control Tr1 emitter, via R4.

A supply of 15v to 20v may be used, and R8 can if necessary be modified to suit other supplies. Input is of quite high impedance (R2 and Tr1) so medium or lower impedance audio sources can be connected directly. Where high impedance inputs are needed, this can be arranged as shown elsewhere.

The amplifier can be incorporated with a mixer or other circuit, or can form a separate unit. A screened case is recommended. Jack sockets will allow the amplifier to be placed in any low-level circuit position as needed with a minimum of difficulty.

Components for 30dB Preamplifier, Figure 4

R1	120k	R2	150k
R3	1.5k	R4	56k
R5	2.2k	R6	330 ohm
R7	270 ohm	R8	1k
C1	0.33 μF	C2, C4,	220 μF
C3	4.7 μF	2 x BC108, etc.	

2-Input FET Mixer

The very high gate input impedance of the field effect transistor enables a preamplifier/mixer to be made with high input impedance. It can be used with crystal microphone and pickup, and also with lower impedance sources.

Input to socket A, Figure 5 is to the volume control VR1, and the input at B is adjusted by VR2. Either can be faded in or out, or set at a wanted level. R1 prevents audio from B being shorted when VR1 is at zero, and in the same way R2 prevents VR2 shorting out signals from A and VR1.

C1 couples to the FET gate. Here, the general purpose type 2N3819 is indicated. Viewing Tr1 as shown, leads are D, G and S. (Drain, Gate and Source). Other FETs can be used, but it is important to employ the correct connections for them. Thus the 2N5457, MPF103, MPF104 and similar types have leads in the order Gate, Source, Drain. The FET is N-channel.

Some modification to component values is possible, without upsetting the circuit operation. A 12v supply is convenient, usually from the main amplifier or other equipment.

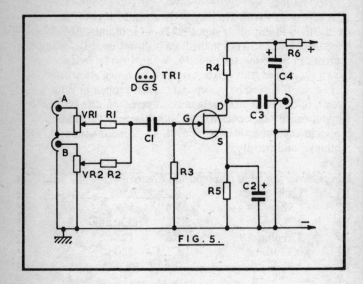

FIG. 5.

Components for 2-Input FET Mixer, Figure 5

VR1, VR2	2 megohm log pots	R1, R2	1.5 megohm
R3	3.3 megohm	R4	4.7k
R5	2.2k	R6	560 ohm
C1	0.1 μF	C2	100 μF
C3	0.47 μF	C4	470 μF
Tr1	2N3819		

Construction is on a small perforated board. R1 and R2 can be soldered directly to the wiper tage of VR1 and VR2. Sockets A and B can be located near these, on the case front.

If the unit is to run from its own battery, place an on-off switch in one battery lead. This is best separated from VR1 or VR2 so that these can be left at previous settings, if the mixer is used as a preamplifier. A "battery on" indicator

10

taking negligble current can be arranged by placing a LED and resistor in series across C4. Connect the LED in the polarity causing it to be lit. The resistor can be about 1k to 2.2k.

Unless used with relatively simple and low power equipment (such as a small battery operated amplifier) a screened case or enclosed box should be used. This is grounded to negative, and avoids picking up hum, or similar difficulties.

3-Input Mixer

Figure 6 is a mixer for three inputs, each with its own level or volume control. By this means, one input may be used as a background for another, or one can be faded while another is brought up.

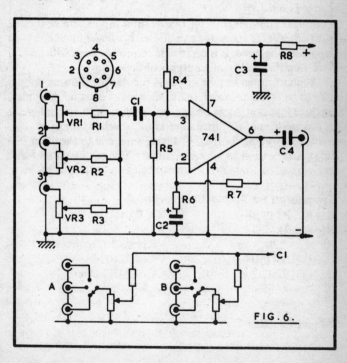

FIG. 6.

11

The inputs are high impedance. Socket 1 has control VR1, socket 2 control VR2, and socket 3 has VR3. Resistors R1, R2 and R3 prevent the short-circuiting of input, with a control at zero. C1 couples to input on the 741 IC amplifier.

In the 741, gain depends on negative feedback by R7, and can be modified by changing R6 or R7. Changing R7 to 47k will reduce gain, while using 100k here will increase it.

A supply of 12v to 24v will usually be convenient, and in some circuits with well smoothed and by-passed supplies C3 and R8 can be omitted.

Leads for the metal can 741 are shown, and these can be arranged to suit the holes of 0.1in and 0.15in matrix perforated boards. Layout should provide good grounds for sockets 1, 2 and 3, and their controls, but avoid long or adjacent leads, or slight unwanted coupling effects may be produced. A screened box, with numbered controls, is recommended.

Similar arrangements, for two or three inputs, can be used with other IC or transistor amplifiers. If a larger number of inputs will be used, it is preferable to provide each with its own amplifier and to mix outputs of these.

A modification to take up to six inputs, but allowing only two to be faded or mixed, is also shown in Figure 6. Any one of three inputs at A can be selected by the 3-way switch here, as can any one of the three inputs at B. Each is subject to individual volume control. Changing from one to the other is by switching from an unwanted input. This can be useful for comparison of alternative sources, such as pickups, tuners, etc.

Components for 3-Input Mixer, Figure 6

R1, R2, R3	270k	R4, R5	100k
R6	1k	R7	56k
R8	2.2k	VR1/2/3	1 megohm log.
C1	0.47 μF	C2	10 μF
C3	220 μF	C4	2.2 μF
IC	741	Sockets, board, etc.	

3-Input Equaliser

Where comprehensive adjustable tone controls are present, a

simplified form of input equaliser may be used, such as that in Figure 7. Here (1) is for ceramic cartridge, (2) for crystal microphone and (3) for radio or tuner input. Switch S1 selects any one input as required.

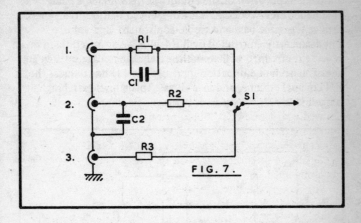

R3 can be modified by trial, depending on the tuner output and amplifier sensitivity.

This type of circuit is easily fitted at the input of any amplifier. Its performance depends somewhat on other circumstances and it is intended to operate into a high impedance.

For best equalisation of various inputs, a circuit having selective feedback can be adopted. Characteristics of this can be improved, and external factors (such as the impedance at S1) can be correct for best operation.

Components for 3-Input Equaliser, Figure 7

R1	1.5 megohm	R2	12k
R3	470k	C1	10pF
C2	6.8pF		

Stereo Input Control

Figure 8 is intended for a high output stereo crystal pickup, but may be used for mono. Adjustable controls are provided for bass, treble, balance and volume.

For mono, the circuit is as shown, except that the balance control VR3 is not required, and a jack for a single audio input can be fitted. For stereo, ganged potentiometers are fitted, allowing duplication of the circuit for right and left hand channels. VR1, VR2 and VR4 operate so that both channels receive the same bass and treble adjustment, and volume is simultaneously controlled by VR4. VR3 is so wired that equal volume is obtained with approximately the middle setting, and adjustment in one direction increases the LH but reduces the RH channel volume, and vice versa. This allows matching output levels.

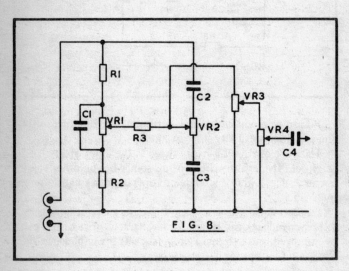

FIG. 8.

The control circuit will be followed by a preamplifier. This could be constructed as a separate stereo (or mono) unit, in a screened case, with output socket for connecting to the main amplifier. Or it might be located at the stereo (or mono) input socket of the main amplifier, where this has sufficient gain.

Components for Stereo Input Control, Figure 8

R1, R2	100k	R3	470k
C1	680pF	C2, C3	270pF
C4	47nF	VR1/2/3/4	2 megohm

14

TBA800 Stereo Amplifier

Further details of the TBA800 appear later. Figure 9 shows
the circuit of a complete stereo amplifier, including power
supply for AC mains. If employed in conjunction with a pick-
up such as the dual-point Sonotone 2509 (turnover stylus) it
can be used with 16 2/3, 33 1/3, 45 and 78 rpm recordings.
With low level sources, a preamplifier will be needed for each
channel.

Input for the right hand channel is at the socket RH, and
with this type of pick-up VR1 and VR4 allow a simplified form
of tone control. VR6 is the volume control.

VR1 and VR2 are a ganged potentiometer. Similarly, VR4
and VR5, and the volume controls VR6 and VR7 operate
together with both right hand and left hand channels. VR3 is
for balance, and is initially set with its wiper at a central position.
It allows the relative volume between RH and LH channels to
be adjusted.

Input is to 8 of the IC from C3, and output for the speaker
is via C19 to socket 1. Negative feedback and audio shaping
are obtained by C15, R13 and the other components here. The
LH channel duplicates that for the RH channel, and output is
to socket 2. Non-reversible sockets are used for correct phasing
of the speaker cones. Each speaker may be 12 ohm. Other
impedances are possible.

Mains transformer T1 has a secondary providing about 18v,
and this will result in about 25v across the main smoothing
capacitor C23. S is a bridge rectifier, or four individual
rectifiers (such as 1N4002) connected to perform an equivalent
function. Operation can be from a lower voltage secondary,
with some reduction in maximum volume.

The indivudual capacitors C21 and C22 are near IC1 and IC2,
to prevent instability. Layout and wiring will keep input
circuits, such as sockets and potentiometers, away from output
and mains circuits and T1. Input circuits are screened in the
usual way.

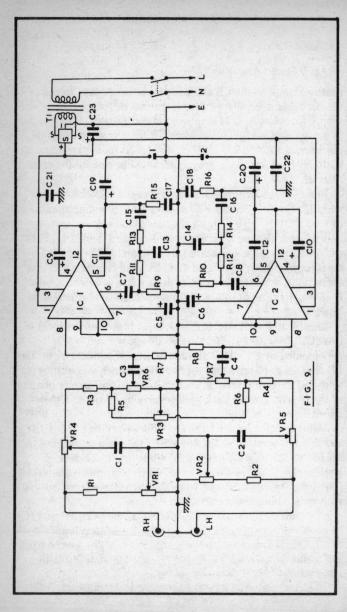

FIG. 9.

16

Components for TBA800 Stereo Amplifier, Figure 9

R1, R2 270k	R3, R4 330k
R5, R6 220k	R7, R8 1 megohm
R9, R10 47 ohm	R11, R12 390 ohm
R13, R14 1.8k	R15, R16 1 ohm
VR1, VR2 2 x 2 meg log.	VR3 2 meg linear
VR4, VR5 2 x 470k linear	VR6, VR7 2 x 2 meg log.
C1, C2 560pF	C3, C4 22nF
C5, C6 100 μF	C7, C8 47 μF
C9, C10 47 μF	C11, C12 220pF
C13, C14 0.33 μF	C15, C16 0.22 μF
C17, C18 0.1 μF	C19, C20 470 μF
C21, C22 0.1 μF	C23 2200 μF
S Silicon bridge rectifier, 50v 1A	
T1 Mains transformer, 18v 1A secondary	
IC1 TBA800	IC2 TBA800

4 IC Stereo Amplifier

Figure 10 shows the method of arranging left hand and right hand channels for a stereo amplifier. LH hand input is to socket 1, and to the preamplifier IC1. This integrated circuit can be a separate IC for each channel, or may be one-half of a dual IC intended to be used as preamplifier for both channels. IC1 has connections and peripheral components to suit.

Output from IC1 is via C1 and R1, to the tone control formed by C3 and VR1, and volume control VR3. The RH channel, with input at socket 2, similarly has the tone control potentiometer VR2, and volume control VR4. VR1/VR2 is a ganged component so that the tone of both channels is adjusted together. In the same way, VR3 and VR4 are ganged, for adjustment of volume. Thus approximately equal signal levels for LH and RH channels are taken from the wipers of VR3 and VR4.

The balance control VR5 operates individually, boosting volume on one channel while reducing it on the other channel. VR5 is originally set with its wiper placed centrally, and is subsequently adjusted as necessary to compensate for lack of balance in the two channels.

C5 couples to the input of the main IC amplifier, IC3 for

the LH channel, and C6 similarly couples IC4 for the RH channel. These ICs will again have external wiring and components to suit, and they deliver their outputs at C7 and C8, for the LH and RH speakers. These connect with some form of non-reversible socket.

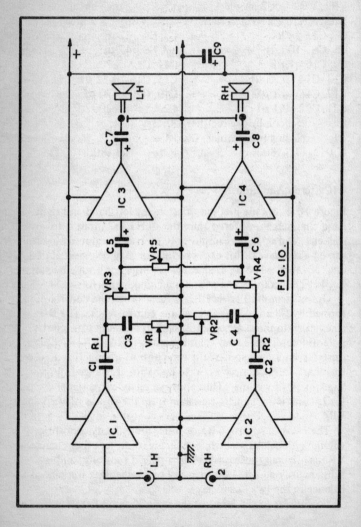

FIG. 10.

A wide range of integrated circuits could be used, depending on the power output wanted, and other features of the amplifier. The preamplifier or main amplifier sections could also be of individual transistor types, instead of ICs.

Both amplifiers operate from a common power supply. Current requirements are about twice those of a single or mono amplifier of power rating equal to that of one channel.

In a typical circuit, it is only necessary to provide details for one channel, as the other duplicates this. Speaker cones must be correctly phased.

Components for 4 IC Stereo Amplifier, Figure 10

C1, C2	10 μF	C3, C4	0.1 μF
C5, C6	2 μF	C7, C8	470 μF
C9	1000 μF	R1, R2	1.5k
VR1/2	2 x 22k linear pot.	VR3/4	2 x 22k log pot.
VR5	22k linear pot.	IC1/2	Preamplifiers
IC3/4	Main amplifiers	Matching speakers	

Class A Workshop Amplifier

An amplifier capable of adequate output for test purposes is a useful item to have to hand, and the circuit in Figure 11 needs very few components. It will operate satisfactorily with quite a wide range of voltage, and with transistors other than those shown.

VR1 is the volume control, and values from 100k to 1 megohm are practical. In some cases this item could be omitted, though it is useful to keep down input when necessary.

R1 supplies base current for Tr1. R2 and VR2 together form the collector load for Tr1, and adjustment of VR2 allows suitable working conditions for Tr2 to be obtained. A transistor with a high current gain is most suitable for Tr1. With other types, the effect of changing R1 to 470k, or 220k, can be tried. R2 is to limit current if VR2 is adjusted to zero resistance.

C1 may be 0.1 μF to 1 μF. C2 and C3 can be 100 μF to 1000 μF. C2 need only be of very low voltage rating, but C3 is 16v, for up to 15v supply.

The 15 ohm speaker is not a midget unit, and can best be

5in or 6in in diameter (say 150mm) or 4 x 7in (102 x 178mm) or larger. It must be mounted in a cabinet. This can also take the amplifier, VR1 and an input jack socket, and a simple power supply unit for AC operation.

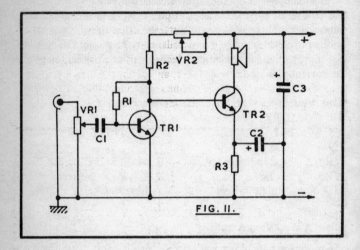

FIG. II.

VR2 is pre-set, when first testing the amplifier. Place a meter on its 100mA or similar range in one supply lead. Begin with the whole of VR2 in circuit. Rotate VR2 until the meter shows about 45mA to 50mA. This should be found to give good volume and reproduction. VR2 can be set for lower currents for battery running, with satisfactory results. A fairly generous current and voltage will increase the power handling capacity of the output stage Tr2, but if current is too high for the transistor, this will overheat, and thermal runaway may begin. This is shown by falling volume and rapidly rising current, and should be halted. VR2 should be set so that this does not happen.

Components for Class A Workshop Amplifier, Figure 11

R1	1 megohm	R2	10k
R3	22 ohm	VR1	220k log pot.
VR2	100k linear pre-set pot	15 ohm speaker	
C1	0.5 μF	C2, C3	1000 μF, etc.

Components for this amplifier can be fitted to a small 0.15in
matrix board, Figure 11B. The foil conductors, on the underside of the board, are only shown where necessary for
components, and must be cut at points X. This is most easily
done with a sharp drill or foil cutter. Check that fragments of
copper do not touch adjacent foils, or remain uncut.

Take red and black flexible leads from positive and negative,
two leads from S—S for speaker, and connect C1 to VR1 wiper
tag, and outer tag to negative line. The remaining outer tag of
VR1 is connected to the audio input socket.

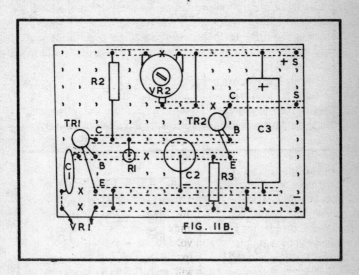

FIG. 11B.

Class A Booster

This amplifier is primarily intended to be driven by a small
receiver such as generally provides some 250mW or so output.
It gives a very considerable increase in volume, for in-car
listening, or other purposes. It will generally run from a 12v
accumulator available in the vehicle, but may be operated from
a power pack able to supply about 12v 1A, or can be run at
reduced power from large dry cells.

When the receiver is to be used with the car in motion, an external aerial, plugged into the outside aerial socket of the radio, is essential. If no such socket is present, a coil having some sixty turns or so of fine gauge wire may be arranged on the ferrite rod (or in some cases adjacent to it) and used for external aerial coupling. Take one end of the winding to the ground line, and the other to the aerial. Where there is no motion, enough signal pick-up should be obtainable from the internal ferrite aerial, though the receiver may need to be near a window, or located with a particular bearing because of aerial directivity.

In Figure 12 audio signals are taken from a transformer coupled 8 ohm earphone socket of the receiver. A shielded cable is worthwhile here unless it is very short. In this way, audio signals drive Tr1 base, and the receiver transformer winding provides the bias DC circuit to positive of C1 and to the wiper of VR1.

Output transformer or tapped choke T1 is required because the usual speaker will not be able to handle the collector current, for full power. T1 should have a low DC resistance. The secondary of a mains transformer intended to deliver 2v,

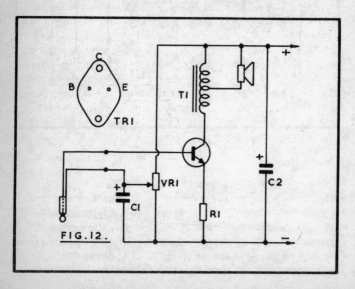

FIG.12.

6v and 12v at 1A was found suitable here. Using 0v and 12v taps for collector and positive, a 3 ohm speaker operated satisfactorily from the 6v and 12v taps, though a unit with 8 ohm impedance was reasonably successful. With insufficient loading (speaker of too high impedance) distortion set in rapidly with increased volume. Primary leads or tags must not touch each other or other items.

VR1 is initially set with its wiper near negative, and is adjusted until collector current, with no signal, is about 400mA to 600mA. For dry batteries, it can be set to about 100mA, with a reduction in maximum volume obtainable. VR1 may be 100 ohm, with a 100 ohm resistor from its upper tag to positive. R1 may be two 2.2 ohm resistors in parallel.

Components for Class A Booster, Figure 12

R1	1 ohm 1w	VR1	250 ohm wire-wound pot.
C1	220 μF	C2	1500 μF
Tr1	2N3055	T1	as text.

Tr1 must be fitted to a heat sink, and its case is common to the collector. It is in order to use the insulation set (mica washer and bushes) and fit Tr1 to the chassis or case; or to use a separate heat sink, with Tr1 bolted directly to it, and to insulate the sink from other items. Base and emitter pins pass through clearance holes, and all burr should be removed from these and the fixing holes, to obtain good thermal contact. Various components can be tried at T1, but the winding should be of low resistance, of reasonably stout guage, and the ratio generally between 4:1 to 2:1. This depends somewhat on the current level set by VR1.

Transformer Coupled Amplifier

Circuits needing no transformers are now most popular, but the working of a transformer coupled amplifier will become clear from Figure 13 and equipment needing attention may use similar circuits. If transformers are to hand, it may be convenient to utilise these to make a useful stand-by amplifier.

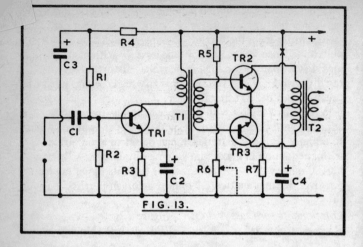

FIG. 13.

Audio input is at C1. Tr1 is an amplifier/driver. Base conditions are set by R1 and R2, and emitter bias by R3. R4 and C3 decouple the base supply and possibly the supply to earlier stages.

The driver transformer T1 has a centre-tapped secondary, so driving the bases of Tr2 and Tr3 out of phase. Tr2 is driven more into conduction for one half of the audio cycle, and Tr3 for the other half. This allows good power output to be realised. The signals are taken to transformer T2, which has a centre-tapped primary, and are here combined, to couple to a low impedance speaker. C4 is a by-pass capacitor.

Bias conditions for Tr2 and Tr3 depend on R5 and R6. These may be accurately selected resistors, to suit Tr2 and Tr3. Or R6 may be preset. If so, use the minimum value at R6 which results in satisfactory volume and reproduction, but without excess collector current. If a meter is placed to read collector current at X (or if preferred in series with the battery, allowing for earlier stages) R6 can usually be set so that current is 5mA to 15mA or so, with no signal, peaks rising to 25mA to 75mA with good volume. If R6 is low in value, objectionable crossover distortion arises; if too high in value, quiescent (no signal) current is too heavy.

R7 is the common emitter resistor. NPN transistors have a

24

negative emitter line. Where PNP transistors are fitted, this line is positive, and polarity of C2, C3 and C4 will be reversed.

Negative feedback, often by a single high value resistor, may be taken from one output transistor collector. Sometimes feedback is from T2 secondary.

Such amplifiers generally are for about 200mW to 1 watt, but may be for much larger outputs. Typical values for a small audio amplifier for 9v to 12v use are given below. Many transistor types may be used. Values for Tr1 should allow this to operate correctly as a Class A amplifier. Tr2 and Tr3 should for preference be a matched pair.

Components for Transformer Coupled Amplifier, Figure 13

R1	47k	R2	15k
R3	1k	R4	680 ohm
R5	1.2k	R6	100 ohm; or 250
R7	4.7 ohm		ohm pre-set
C1	0.47 μF	C2	100 μF
C3	100 μF	C4	220 μF
T1	5:1 + 1 etc.	T2	4 + 4:1 etc.

Tr1, Tr2, Tr3, BC108, etc.

Board Layout

Assembly on a plain 0.15in matrix perforated board 16 x 11 holes is shown in Figure 13B. A larger board will be necessary for non-miniature transformers.

If transformers of unknown type are to hand, primary and secondary windings can be located with a testmeter. Windings will be of low DC resistance, but there will be no connection from primary to secondary. A centre-tapped winding will show approximately the same resistance from centre-tap to each end, and twice this value overall. The approximate ratio at 50Hz or 60Hz can be found, if necessary, by supplying low voltage AC from a mains transformer to one winding, with a series limiting resistor in circuit. Then measure the voltages of primary and secondary with an AC meter. This gives the approximate turns ratio. Thus if 6v AC is found across the primary and 1.5v AC across the secondary, the ratio is 6:1.5 or 4:1. The primary and secondary tags or leads may not be placed as in Figure 13B.

As such circuits can use small components for 250mW or

less, or larger items and higher voltage for several watts, layouts and values can be adjusted to suit. It may be possible to repair such an amplifier if defective, or use items to hand. For a new amplifier, a transformerless or IC circuit would normally be used.

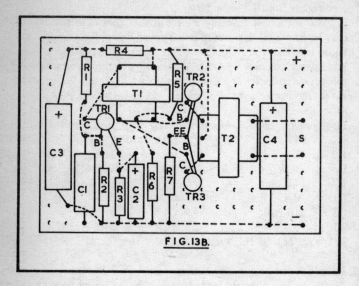

FIG.13B.

Complementary Push-Pull Amplifier

This type of circuit requires no audio transformer, and is used over a wide power range. Figure 14 is a typical circuit, which may be used to amplify signals from a tuner and other purposes.

C1 is the coupling and isolating capacitor, and audio signals can be from a preamplifier, tuner, or other source able to provide a fairly large output. For use with a pick-up, an additional transistor could be used, to drive Tr1. R1 and R2, in conjunction with the supply voltage for R1, set base operating conditions for Tr1.

The collector of Tr1 drives Tr2 and Tr3. Tr3 is a PNP transistor, and Tr2 is NPN. Thus Tr3 is driven into conduction with negative half cycles, and Tr2 with positive half cycles. Voltage drop in R4 provides a quiescent or no-signal bias for the output pair.

26

Emitter resistors R5 and R6 help stabilise operating conditions. Feedback from the junction of these resistors to R1 and Tr1 base also provides overall stabilisation of the directly coupled stages.

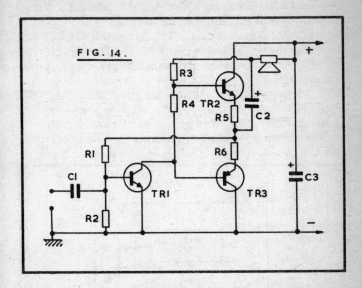

FIG. 14.

Quiescent current and operating conditions are considerably influenced by R4. When using a different complementary pair for Tr2 and Tr3, the value of this resistor in particular may need changing. The speaker is 8 ohm. As with IC amplifiers, a speaker of lower than the specified minimum impedance should not be used, or damage to the output stage can be caused when operating this at maximum power. With reduced voltage, as in Figure 14, damage is unlikely, but too much change in speaker impedance will result in loss of volume.

Components for Complementary Push-Pull Amplifier, Figure 14

R1, R2	220k	R3	680 ohm
R4	47 ohm	R5, R6	2.2 ohm
C1	0.47 µF	C2, C3	220 µF
Tr1	BC149	Tr2	AC176
Tr3	AC128		

Figure 14B shows assembly of the amplifier on 0.15 in matrix board, 17 x 10 holes in size, with foils running horizontally. These are only shown where they complete circuits between components, for clarity. Make a foil break between C1 and R5, either with the cutter available for this purpose, or with a few turns with a sharp drill.

A BC109 fits most readily at Tr1, though it is not difficult to arrange the layout here to take a BC149. The transistors are suited to work together, so that changes to any one may require some modification to resistor values. AC176/AC128 output pairs, and many similar transistors, are easily obtainable. Tr2 must of course be NPN, and Tr3 PNP types, and results are most satisfactory when they are matched for use together.

Where input is by means of a screened lead, take the outer

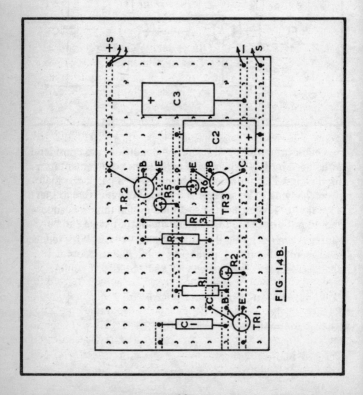

FIG. 14B.

braid to the negative line near Tr1, and inner conductor to C1.

With other transistors, R1 can be modified in value so that
negative of C2 takes up approximately a half-voltage position,
as shown by a high resistance meter, with no signal. R4 can
be such that crossover distortion is avoided, but without a
heavy resting current. Increasing R4 raises current. Some
5mA to 10mA or so will usually be suitable, rising to 25mA
to 50mA or so with good volume.

Printed Circuit 3-Stage Amplifier

This amplifier provides high gain, and will be suitable for many
general purposes where an output of about ½w is adequate. It
is sufficiently economical to run from a 9v battery.

VR1 is the input gain control, Figure 15. Tr1 is a preamplifier, with base current from R1, and R2 as collector load.
The supply for this stage is decoupled by C3 and R3.

C2 couples to Tr2 base, potential here being set by the
divider R4/R5. Tr2 drives the complementary pair, Tr3 and Tr4,
directly, in the usual type of push-pull circuit requiring no
transformer. Bias for Tr3 and Tr4 is developed across R6.
There is feedback by R7 from the speaker circuit S. R4 is
also returned to the junction of the emitter resistors R8 and
R9, to stabilise DC operating conditions of Tr2, Tr3 and Tr4.
C5 couples audio output to the speaker.

A 15 ohm or 16 ohm unit is suitable. Current drain is
then about 40mA to 60mA at good volume, and about 8mA
to 10mA or so with no signals. Higher impedance and higher
resistance loads can be connected at S, including headphones
of some hundreds of ohms resistance. Peak power and current
are reduced, but will in any case not normally be wanted for
headphones.

The input socket is suitable for general purposes, and
especially medium or low impedances. It can be arranged for
high impedance input as shown elsewhere.

A simple form of top-cut tone control could be connected
from Tr1 base to negative line. Where inputs are too large so
that VR1 is almost at zero, and critical to adjust because volume
is too great, a fixed resistor may be placed between VR1 and
the input socket, or between VR1 wiper and C1.

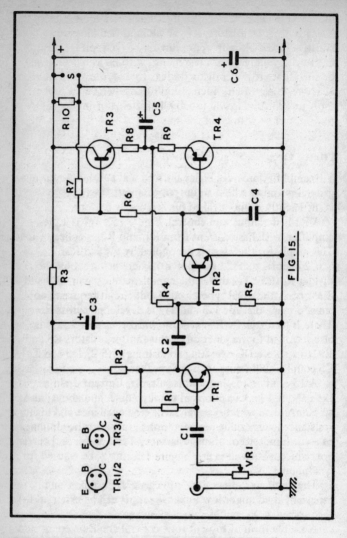

Components for 3-Stage Amplifier, Figure 15

R1	1.8 megohm	R2	8.2k
R3	1.5k	R4	270k
R5	220k	R6	47 ohm

R7	680 ohm	R8, R9	2.2 ohm
R10	1.5k	VR1	100k log pot.
C1	0.1 μF	C2	0.47 μF
C3	125 μF	C4	2.2nF
C5	470 μF	C6	470 μF
Tr1	BC109	Tr2	BC108
Tr3	AC176	Tr4	AC128

The underside of the circuit board for this amplifier is shown in Figure 15B. Connecting points for VR1 are to A and B. Tr1 is at this end of the board. Position emitter, base and collector leads to reach the holes E, B and C. Note polarity of C3, positive to R3. Driver Tr2 follows. R8 and R9 fit vertically on the board, and also R10.

Solder on a red wire for positive, black for negative, and two green leads for speaker, from S–S. Board dimensions are not too important, but 4 x 2in (102 x 51mm) will be convenient.

It is best not to bend resistor leads extremely sharply against the body, as this may partly fracture the wire. Solder must flow round the lead and on the foil, to form a correct joint. Excess wire is then cut off. Transistor wires should not be heated for longer than required.

The amplifier is intended to fit a case with sockets and VR1 on the front, and taking also a 9v battery, or a holder with six 1.5v cells. Three 6ba bolts fix the board to the bottom of the case. These should be long enough for all joints and leads to clear the case, and each bolt will require three nuts, to allow locking to case and board. Two bolts also provide grounding of the board negative line to the metal case. More details on board preparation appear in Figure 18B.

Typical voltage readings for the amplifier, using a 10k/V meter on a 10v range, are as follows. These can vary within reasonable limits, without upsetting results. Tr1 base 0.4v. Tr1 collector 3.25v. C3 positive 8v. Tr2 base 0.6v. Tr2 collector 4.5v. C5 negative, 4.6v. C6 positive 9v.

31

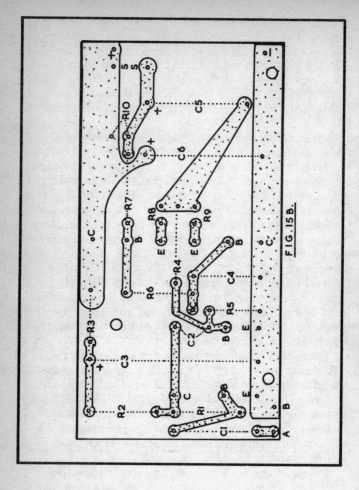

FIG. 15 B.

4-Transistor Amplifier

This amplifier will deliver approximately 3 watts and can be driven by a high output crystal cartridge pick-up, or equivalent input from a tuner or preamplifier.

The circuit has amplifier, driver and complementary push-pull output, Figure 16. C1 may be taken to the wiper of a 100k volume control, or to a control whose value depends on

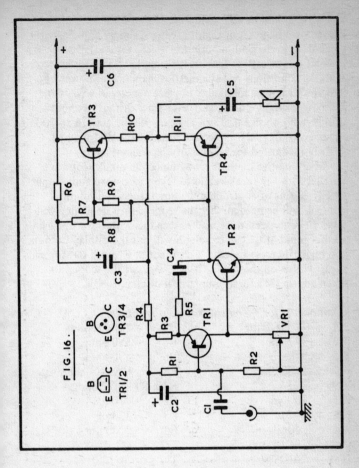

FIG.16.

the input provided, or to a top-cut type tone control. If an
IC or transistor preamplifier is incorporated, for additional
sensitivity, the circuit here can be arranged to suit.

Direct current feedback is provided from the output circuit,
by R4, to R1, to stabilise working conditions. Audio feedback
here is avoided by C2. Tr1 collector provides base input for
Tr2, which in turn drives Tr4 and Tr3. Thermistor R8, in
parallel with the resistor R9, helps stabilise working conditions.

For full output a 12 ohm speaker is used, and 22v supply.

33

The PSU should be able to deliver at least 200mA. A 15 ohm speaker can be used, or slightly reduced supply voltage, with some drop in maximum output.

VR1 allows setting the directly-coupled stages for correct working conditions and symmetrical handling of power by Tr3 and Tr4. One method is to place a meter in series with the power supply line and set VR1 for a current of about 25mA, with no signal. Current peaks will be 100mA to 200mA or so, according to volume, and if necessary VR1 may be slightly readjusted for satisfactory reproduction.

An alternative method is to connect an oscilloscope in parallel with the speaker, and to take a sine wave audio input to C1. Means of controlling the input, such as a volume control, will be needed. Set the scope at any frequency which gives an easily seen trace, and reduce this with the scope gain so that input at C1 can be raised, without the display becoming too high. Increase the sine wave input at C1 until flat-topping is just visible on the scope. If necessary set the scope gain. Then adjust VR1 for a symmetrical display.

Components for 4-Transistor Amplifier, Figure 16

R1	1 megohm	R2	1.8 megohm
R3	47 ohm	R4	680 ohm
R5	1k	R6	390 ohm
R7	180 ohm	R8	VA1077 thermistor
R9	22 ohm	R10, R11	2.2 ohm
C1	0.1 μF	C2	470 μF
C3	47 μF	C5	220 μF
C4	40nF	C6	2200 μF
Tr1	BC157	Tr2	BC148
Tr3	AC176*	Tr4	AC128*

12 ohm speaker
*Heat sinks 5 x 7mm, 1.5mm aluminium

Construction will most easily be on a plain perforated board. The heat sinks can be fashioned from aluminium sheet, with a flange bolted to the board.

Disposition of components can resemble their location in the theoretical circuit. It is important to provide a stout, low impedance ground line, especially between negative power input point, speaker, Tr4, and C6 negative.

LM386 Amplifier

This audio IC operates from low voltage, and is suitable for
modest speaker volume (250mW), or headphones. Figure 17
shows the IC connections and circuit, and very few additional
components are needed.

There is some latitude in values, but a speaker of under 8
ohm impedance is not recommended. A typical battery supply
would be 9v. C1 and C2 have some effect on tonal quality.
C4 can be omitted with some supplies.

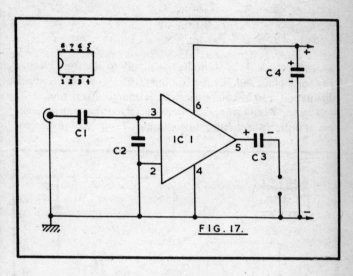

FIG. 17.

Components for LM386 Amplifier, Figure 17

C1	0.47 µF	C2	270pF
C3	470 µF	C4	470 µF
IC1	LM386	8 ohm speaker	

LM380 Amplifiers

The LM380 is a versatile IC amplifier, and can be used with
supplies of from 9v to 22v. Power output is about 2.5 watt

with 18v, and proportionately lower with reduced voltages. This makes it suitable for many applications.

The IC incorporates self protection against some forms of misuse. It has output circuit short protection, and automatic cut-out if overheated. For maximum output, heat-sinking via the circuit board or similar means is required, and output is limited to about 1.25W with no sink.

Approximate typical output powers, loads, and voltages are as follows:

4 ohm speaker	*8 ohm speaker*	*16 ohm speaker*
9v 1.25w	12v 1.5w	16v 1.5w
10v 1.5w	16v 2.75w	20v 2.75w
12v 2w	20v 3.5w	
14v 2.75w		

Dissipation in the IC limits the supply to 10v for 4 ohm, 14v for 8 ohm, and 20v for 16 ohm speakers. Momentary peak dissipations can of course exceed continuous dissipation.

Figure 18 is an amplifier circuit suitable for a ceramic pick-up, or input from a radio tuner, and for a supply of up to 16v.

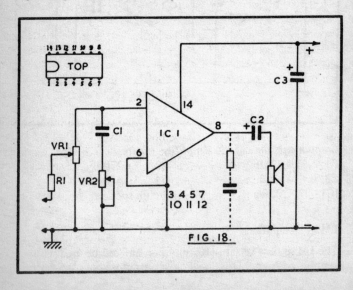

FIG. 18.

VR1 is the gain or volume control, and VR2 a simple form of tone control. A circuit board with an extended foil area to which 3, 4, 5, 10, 11 and 12 can be soldered will provide some measure of heat sinking.

Supply polarity must not be reversed. If the supply has ripple causing hum, a by-pass capacitor of about 4.7 μF can be taken from pin 1 to negative line. C3 should be adjacent to the IC. Where layout or external circuits cause oscillation or instability, a capacitor of 47nF to 0.1 μF may be connected from 8 to negative, at the IC. Except for low voltage use, the resistor and capacitor shown as optional are included, and can be 2.7 ohm and 0.1 μF.

Voltage gain is about 34db, so a preamplifier is required for low-level signals. The IC alone is not suitable for microphone use. The preamplifier may be transistor or IC, and circuits will be found elsewhere.

Components for LM380N Amplifier, Figure 18

VR1	22k	VR2	10k
C1	50nF	C2	470 μF 16v
C3	470 μF 16v	16 ohm speaker	

Printed Circuit (LM380)

Various forms of construction can be used, as shown elsewhere. Generally, plain perforated boards can be adopted, and wired on the underside; or boards with foils may be chosen, these being used as conductors, and cut where required. It is also fairly easy to make a printed circuit board especially for the project.

To make a board of this kind, a drawing or diagram should first be prepared. Figure 18B is a board for the LM380 amplifier. Crossovers on top of the board are generally arranged by components themselves, as foils for other circuits can pass below these. With more complicated boards, some wired connections may be used, to enable the required circuits to be made without roundabout or awkward routes.

In Figure 18B a large area of foil is left for pins 3—7 and 10—12, for heat sink purposes. This is also the negative line. Reasonably wide areas of foil are best for negative lines or returns. Elsewhere, and particularly where current is low,

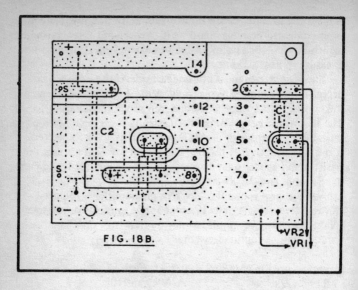

FIG. 18B.

very narrow foils can be used. Input and output circuits are
kept clear of each other, just as with a wired amplifier.

After arranging components suitably, an actual size layout
is made. A piece of perforated board will be useful to help
locate hole positions, especially for ICs.

Instructions for preparation and etching can be obtained
with the required materials. The foil must be perfectly clean.
Those areas to be left intact are painted over with an etch
resistant fluid applied with a small brush. For finer lines and
small areas, a type of felt tipped pen is available. The whole
board is then immersed in etching solution (which must be
mixed and used according to the maker's instructions) until
the unprotected foil is dissolved. The board is then washed
and dried. The protective varnish may need scraping off
where leads are to be soldered. Holes for these are made with
a small drill.

Some correction to an imperfect, home-produced board of
this kind is possible. If unnoticed streaks of varnish have
resulted in narrow conductive paths, these can be scraped away
with a sharply edged tool. In the same way, a cut can be
provided in a conductor. Again, should some areas have been

etched away due to imperfect protection, or an error, a wired connection can be substituted. With reasonable care, no such work should be needed, but it may save a board which is otherwise perfect.

In Figure 18B holes are provided for speaker, positive, negative, and potentiometer leads. VR1 and VR2 will be near the board. The speaker leads may run to sockets. The resistor and capacitor from 8 of the IC to earth line are included.

TBA800 Amplifier

This IC requires more external components, but has greater sensitivity, which may be set by the value of the feedback resistor, R1 in the circuit, Figure 19. Operation is typically from 9v to 24v, and maximum output is 4.5w.

Operating conditions and loads are approximately as follows:

8 ohm speaker	16 ohm speaker
9v 0.75w	9v 0.5w
12v 2w	12v 1.25w
20v 4w	20v 3w
	24v 4.5w

VR1 is the gain control, and a resistor of 82k may be connected from 8 to 9 where this control is to be omitted, with input controlled elsewhere. The quiescent or no-signal current is low, typically about 5mA to 10mA, rising to 180mA to 300mA for full output.

C2 and C3 help form the frequency response, while C4 is speaker coupling, C5 a by-pass across the supply, and C6 with R2 the Zobel network. If more conveniently available, R2 may be two 2.2 ohm resistors in parallel.

The feedback level active at 6 may be modified by changing R1. With the amplifier operating into an 8 ohm load, typical sensitivity levels for R1 are: 47 ohm 20mV, 100 ohm 40mV, and 150 ohm 60mV, for 1 watt output.

The pins fit 0.1in matrix board, but are staggered and can be arranged to fit 0.15in matrix (IC at 45 degrees). The metal tabs projecting from the IC provide enough heat sink area for·

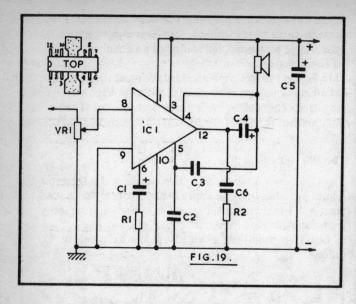

FIG.19.

up to 1 watt. For higher power, they can pass down through slots cut in the board, and be soldered to enlarged foil areas. Or they may be raised, and soldered to a sink above the IC.

As with other audio amplifiers, heat dispersal becomes important with the higher power levels. Heating is reduced if the speaker is at least 16 ohm, with a 12v or similar supply. A wide range of voltages can be used, but care is needed with 20v and over.

Components for TBA800 Amplifier, Figure 19

R1	100 ohm	R2	1 ohm
VR1	100k pot.	C1	100 μF 10v
C2	2.7nF	C3	270pF
C4	470 μF 25v	C5	470 μF 25v
C6	0.1 μF	TBA800	

10W/20W Amplifier

The TDA2020 is a high power integrated circuit, and it allows the construction of an audio amplifier for outputs in the 10

40

watt to 20 watt range with very few other components. External circuits are extremely simple, compared with a 5-transistor or similar amplifier of equal power, Figure 20.

The IC requires a centre-tapped power supply. Equal positive and negative voltages are needed, each side of the zero or grounded line. This is quite readily arranged, as shown later.

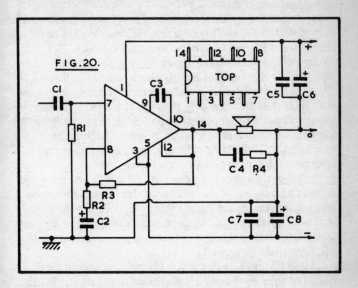

FIG.20.

A range of voltages can be used, depending on the power wanted, and speaker impedance. Using a 4 ohm speaker, supply voltages and approximate power outputs are as follows:

> 12–0–12v   11W
> 16–0–16v   18W
> 18–0–18v   21W

For an 8 ohm speaker, power is slightly reduced:

> 12–0–12v   7W
> 16–0–16v   12W
> 18–0–18v   15W

The absolute maximum is a 20–0–20v supply, and over 18–0–18v is not recommended. The 4 ohm unit is thus necessary for the highest power output, but the 8 ohm speaker will be in order if preferred for lower powers. For reduced power, down to 9v or less may be used.

Sensitivity is around 250mV to 350mV. Direct drive from a tuner or other unit with sufficient output is practicable, though a preamplifier will generally be employed, as with other high-power amplifiers.

Input is to the isolating capacitor C1. C3 is for compensation. Output is from 14, and negative feedback is by means of R3. The values of R2 and C2 also help control feedback. R4 and C4 parallel the loudspeaker, which requires no coupling capacitor. It is possible to modify the values of C1, R1, R2, C2 and R3, to alter input impedance of the circuit, or response.

Quiescent or no-signal current is about 50mA, and maximum power will give current peaks of up to 3.5A or so. Peak current is reduced with an 8 ohm speaker, or reduced voltage and power output. Protection is incorporated in the IC against overheating, but not against excess voltage.

For other than very low power, a heat sink is necessary. A shaped and finned sink is available for this IC, and clamps on a conductive area on it. C3 and other components, which should be as near the IC as possible, must be arranged so that they do not obstruct fitting the sink. For maximum convector cooling, sink fins should be vertical.

C5 and C7 are close to the IC. C6 and C8 may not be needed, if the power supply leads are short and stout. But if these leads need to run some distance, C6 and C8 will be required, in addition to the capacitors in the power supply, to maintain stability (except at much reduced power).

Figure 21 shows two methods of supplying power. That at A is only generally suitable for modest power outputs, allowing testing of the circuit from an ordinary PSU. R1 and R2 are of equal value, and their resistance should be as low as possible, and will thus depend on the current available from the PSU, and its voltage. As example, if the PSU could provide 25v at 2A, this would allow a 12½-0-12½v supply to be obtained. If R1 and R2 were each 18 ohm 10w, bleeder current would be about 700mA, leaving rather over 1A for the amplifier. As the voltage lines fluctuate with power drawn, attempts to use this method at full power are not recommended, but it is feasible

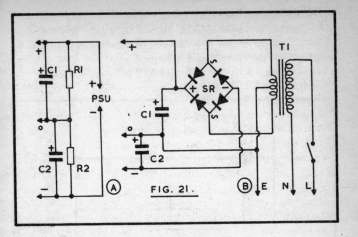

FIG. 21.

as a substitute with the limits mentioned.

At B a transformer with a 12–0–12v 3A secondary will provide about 16v to 18v after rectification. C1 and C2 can be 4700 μF, 20v. Four silicon rectifiers, 50v 3A or similar types, will be satisfactory or a bridge rectifier can be fitted.

The low voltage power supply leads should be stout and short. Care must be taken to observe polarity.

Components for 10W/20W Amplifier, Figure 20

C1	0.22 μF	C2	4.7 μF
C3	68pF	C4, C5, C7	0.1 μF
C6, C8	150 μF or larger	R1, R3	100k
R2	3.3k	R4	1 ohm
TDA2020 with heat sink		4 ohm or 8 ohm speaker	

IC Push-Pull Amplifier

Some integrated circuit amplifiers have available inverting and non-inverting inputs, either of which may be used. With a single IC, one input is often used for the signal, and the other for negative feedback. To obtain approximately double the maximum output power, two ICs can be used, with inputs arranged so that outputs are in push-pull. Figure 22 is a circuit of this type.

Audio input is through R1 and C1, from the preamplifier, tone control, or earlier circuit. An isolating capacitor may be present, and C1 is then unnecessary, but should be included if various units may be plugged in here.

Signal input is to 2 of IC1, and 6 of IC2. At IC1, 6 is

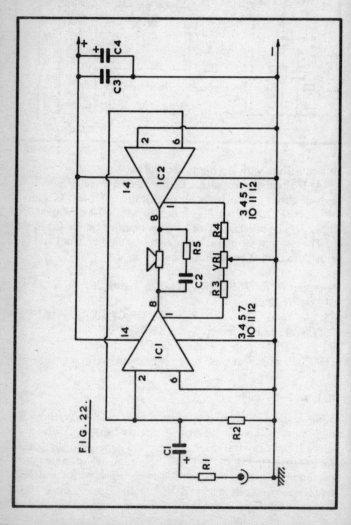

F I G. 22.

grounded, while 2 is grounded at IC2. Outputs at 8—8 are thus in opposite phase. Coupling capacitors are not required, as these points should be at the same potential under no-signal conditions. C2 and R5 are the usual speaker network.

Balance is obtained by means of VR1. This is first set with its wiper in a central position. A meter with a fairly high current range is placed between 8 of one IC and the speaker. Initially, a reduced voltage can be applied to the circuit, or a resistor can be included in the positive line. With no audio signal input, VR1 is adjusted for the least or zero meter reading, showing that voltages at 8—8 have been trimmed to be equal.

Operating conditions for the LM380 have been given, and this amplifier will require approximately twice the power, for full output. C3 should be near the ICs, to suppress HF instability. It may be possible to omit C4, if the power supply leads are short, and a similar capacitor is present in the power supply itself. If not, this component (2200 μF to 4700 μF) will probably be required.

Components for IC Push-Pull Amplifier, Figure 22

R1	1k	R2	2.2k
R3, R4	100k	R5	2.7 ohm
C1	4.7 μF	C2, C3	0.1 μF
C4	4700 μF	VR1	470k linear pot.
IC1, IC2	LM380	8 ohm speaker	

Audio Sources

The source of audio frequency signals, which forms the input to an amplifier, will usually be important. It can be necessary to have in mind the impedance, frequency characteristics, and probable output available to feed into the amplifier. Typically, situations arise where an inexpensive (but high output) pickup is replaced by one of superior type, and volume is then found to be inadequate; or where a microphone is obtained for use with an amplifier employed with a tuner and turntable unit, and is found unsatisfactory.

Exact specifications cannot be given, because these vary between different models, but a general outline of what to expect is possible and will help in providing satisfactory working conditions.

A comprehensive preamplifier or amplifier will have a number of input sockets or channels, to suit various sources.

Radio Tuner
A sensitivity of about 150mV to 250mV would generally be suitable. If the amplifier input is very sensitive the volume control may need to be so near minimum adjustment is unnecessarily difficult. A series resistor is often fitted at this input socket, to reduce sensitivity. Input impedance can be about 500k.

Crystal Pickup
Sensitivity can be about 100mV to 350mV or higher, with about 200mV to 250mV fairly usual. Input impedance can be about 1 megohm. Attenuation of input is needed, except where tuner and pickup are intended for high output, working into an amplifier of modest gain.

Ceramic Cartridge
Expected sensitivity is about 60mV, with up to 200mV or more for high output types. Impedance can be 1 megohm.

Magnetic Pickup

Sensitivity about 1mV to 5mV, and input impedance of about 47k. Adequate gain is necessary to obtain full output from an amplifier when the input is so low.

Tape

A sensitivity of about 250mV to 300mV or so, and impedance of about 500k, will generally be suitable.

Microphones

These also vary considerably between models of the same type, A magnetic microphone can have a sensitivity of 3.5mV, and impedance of 22k. Low cost crystal microphones have an output of about 5mV to 10mV. High output models are available. They require a high impedance circuit and 1 megohm can be used. Dynamic microphones are made in single and dual impedance, or with 50 ohm, 600 ohm, 50k and other impedances for the same type.

Other microphones include highly directional types, ribbon units, hand-held mikes with push-to-talk switches, wide frequency response crystal units for very high impedance (4.7 megohm) and desk, stand, hanging and other units. Data can be obtained from their makers.

If a microphone, pickup or other source intended to operate into a high impedance load is connected to a low impedance, there will be a deterioration in frequency response. This explains the need for high impedance input sockets for some circuits.

Equalising

A preamplifier intended for best results with several types of input will have both sensitivity and tonal balance correcting circuits. These are designed to provide a suitable attenuation and boost, so that the overall frequency response is more level. It is usual to have different networks for disc, tape, etc.

Where fully variable tone controls are fitted, the user can of course adjust these to obtain the type of reproduction which he favours. Settings of the controls can be logged for radio, various tape speeds, and other purposes.

Most equalising circuits use selective negative feedback. A switch may select various component values, to suit radio tuner, magnetic pickup, crystal pickup, or other inputs to be used.

Easy Treble-Bass-Volume Control Circuit

Figure 23 shows a circuit for a crystal pickup, requiring few components, but offering separate control of treble and bass. A volume control is included, and the circuit can be placed at the input point of a preamplifier, or main amplifier of sufficient sensitivity.

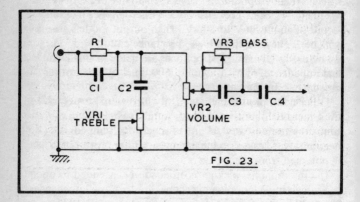

FIG. 23.

C1 provides some treble emphasis, and VR1 is the adjustable top cut control, as the reactance of C2 falls with an increase in frequency. VR2 is the volume control.

VR3 is for bass control, and C4 couples to the base of the first transistor, or IC audio amplifier. Such circuits do not allow shaping of audio response to the extent achieved with more complicated methods, but can give a satisfactory performance. Treble-bass controls offering extremes of boost and attenuation can seldom be employed over their full range. With simplified controls, there is a greater need to adjust volume as well as response. In this way a bass boost may be obtained by reducing treble and increasing gain with the volume control. The overall result is then a strengthening of lower frequencies.

The few components in Figure 23 may be assembled

directly on the potentiometers. If made as a separate unit, a screened box is needed.

Components for Easy Treble-Bass-Volume Control, Figure 23

R1	1 megohm	C1	330pF
C2	4.7nF	C3	2.2nF
C4	0.22 μF	VR1	50k log
VR2	50k log	VR3	100k 1in

Passive Tone Control

This is separate from any power supplies, and is placed in the audio circuit. The most suitable position is between pre-amplifier and main amplifier.

VR1 is for treble (Figure 24) and VR2 for bass. It is feasible to use linear, semi-log or log potentiometers here. Reproduction is approximately flat with the controls central, and both treble and bass can be cut or boosted separately.

VR3 is the volume control. It is convenient to have this in the tone control unit so that adjustments for volume as well as tone are situated together. As is usual with such circuits, there is some overall loss of signal strength, so the preamplifier or

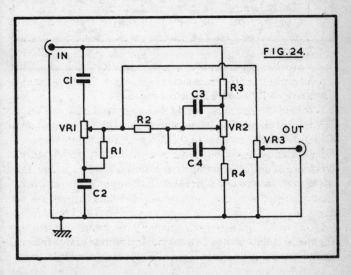

main amplifier controls must be set to compensate for this.

Such a circuit could be included at the input of the main amplifier. When built as a separate unit, it should be in an enclosed metal case, for screening purposes. Jack sockets to match up with other equipment will allow it to be placed in circuit in a few moments. The resistors and capacitors can be grouped round the potentiometers and soldered directly to these and the input socket, and a circuit board is not required, Figure 24B. Some modification of values is feasible.

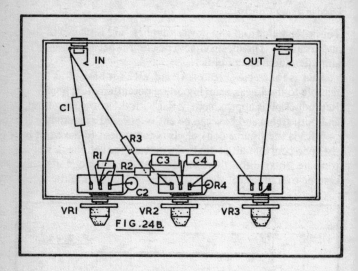

FIG.24B.

Components for Passive Tone Control, Figure 24

R1	100k	R2	100k
R3	150k	R4	15k
C1	270pF	C2	3.3nF
C3	1nF	C4	10nF

VR1/2/3 470k (500k suitable), 2 sockets.
Metal box. Knobs and scales.

Active Tone Control

Figure 25 is the circuit of a tone control with selective feed-back from the collector of Tr1. VR1 is the treble control and

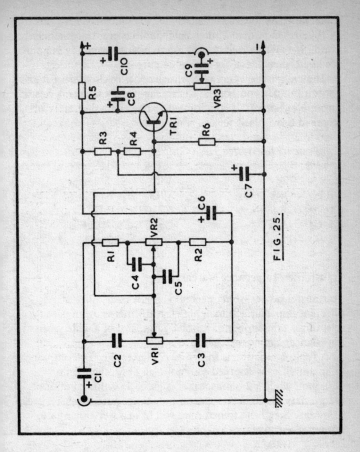

FIG. 25.

input to the base of Tr1 is obtained from C1 and C2, while feedback for these frequencies to VR1 is by C6 and C3. VR1 thus allows adjustment from maximum treble input to Tr1 base with minimum feedback (treble boost) to minimum treble input and maximum feedback (treble cut) conditions.

VR2 operates in a similar manner for bass, with R1 to signal input line and R2 to the feedback coupling capacitor C6. VR3 is a volume control, and if omitted audio signals are taken from C8.

R3, R4 and R6 set the base working conditions of Tr1, and

R5 is the collector load. Values here are for BC108, but BC148, BC107, 2N3704/6 and other small audio types can generally be fitted. If bias conditions need modification, generally R6 only need be changed.

The circuit allows comprehensive control, with 9db cut and boost at 10kHz and 100Hz, so can adequately fill many needs for a tone control. If constructed as a separate unit, a screened box is used.

Components for Active Tone Control, Figure 25

R1, R2	47k	R3, R4	150k
R5	22k	VR1	220k linear
VR2	470k linear	VR3	20k log.
C1	6.8 μF	C2, C3	2.2nF
C4, C5	6.8nF	C6, C7, C8	10μF
C9	6.8 μF	C10	220 μF

Transformer Impedance Matching

To transfer power from one audio circuit to another of different impedance, a matching transformer is often used. By selecting a transformer of suitable ratio, any of a wide range of impedances can be matched.

A typical situation is shown at A, Figure 26. The output stage of an amplifier is assumed to require an optimum load of 450 ohm, while a 2 ohm speaker is used. For this condition, the primary P will have a greater number of turns than secondary S and the transformer will have a step-down ratio, primary to secondary.

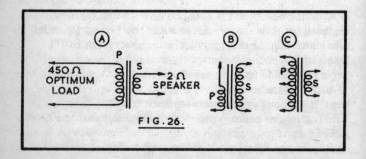

FIG. 26.

B is the reversed situation. A low impedance source is to be connected to the primary P, while the secondary S is to operate into the input of a high-impedance amplifier stage. Here, the transformer will have a step-up ratio.

For A, the transformer ratio can be found from:

$$\sqrt{\frac{\text{Optimum load}}{\text{Speaker impedance}}}$$

With the example given, optimum load was 450 ohm, and speaker impedance 2 ohm, so $450/2 = 225$ and $\sqrt{225} = 15$. The ratio is thus 15:1.

The ratio for other circuits may be found in the same way. Divide the greater impedance by the lesser impedance, and find the square root. As example, for B, operating a 15 ohm microphone into an amplifier with 20k input impedance would call for a 35:1 ratio. As explained, here the low impedance winding is primary.

The transformer at C has a centre-tapped primary. It could be employed to match push-pull output transistors or valves to a speaker. Actual components for such purposes could have an overall primary to secondary ratio of 2:1 or less to 50:1 or higher, depending on optimum load or anticipated load, and speaker impedance. A transformer with an overall primary to secondary ratio of 7:1 could be specified as 3.5 + 3.5:1; or as 7CT:1.

Speaker or other transformers may have a number of tappings, so that a selection of ratios can be provided. A data sheet may indicate which to use for various impedances.

A transformer may have more than one primary or secondary, or may have halves of a winding isolated for bias or other purposes. It is then necessary to assure that the half windings are operated in the correct phase, as for example in the transformer driven single-ended type of stage.

In addition to having a suitable ratio, a transformer must be of sufficient current or power handling capacity. Very small components can be adequate for miniature receivers or similar purposes where power is small (probably under 200mW). Slightly more generous sizes are needed for up to 1 watt or so, and where transformers have to be used for high powers, they become very large and weighty.

Transistor and intergrated circuit amplifiers now largely avoid the need for output matching transformers, but they will be found in much equipment of earlier design.

Resistive Matching

For convenience, an improvement in matching may be obtained in some circuits by adding resistance to raise the impedance. This results in a loss of sensitivity or power, but amplification may be readily available to compensate for this, and the use of a transformer is avoided.

One application is in an amplifier input circuit, Figure 27. At A input is for low impedance. R1, R2 and Tr1 load the input circuit, and the volume control VR1 is also of relatively low value.

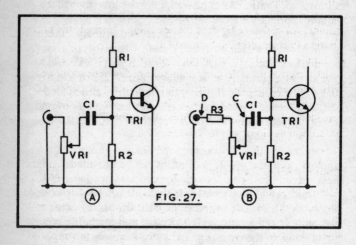

FIG. 27.

For a high input impedance, VR1 is raised in value. But with VR1 at maximum volume position R1 and R2 in A would load the input. A measure of compensation for this is obtained by placing R3 in circuit, B. Input impedance can then be maintained in the vicinity of 500k, for a crystal pick-up, but will be over 1 megohm at low settings of VR1.

With typical driver and output stages following Tr1,

sensitivity could be about 3mV to 5mV at point C, and around 500mV at point D. Removing R3, or reducing it in value, would greatly increase maximum sensitivity from the 500mV level. Loading of a high impedance pick-up by a low impedance input circuit would however cause a deterioration in frequency response.

Other forms of resistive matching may be used at input points, or between units. They may be present with some inputs of a mixer, but not others.

Resistive matching of output circuits is occasionally used. These result in a loss of power. This power loss may not be important when more than adequate power will remain available. Thus if 8 ohm headphones were to be used with an amplifier which must not have an output load of under 16 ohms, the 16 ohm load could be made up by 8 ohm phones and an 8 ohm resistor in series. Normally easily enough volume would be anticipated. But approximately half the output power would be lost in the resistor, so this would not be suitable for ordinary loudspeaker working. Instead, the correct 16 ohm unit would then be needed.

Similar considerations apply to using a reproducer and resistor in parallel. Medium or high impedance headphones with a suitable parallel resistor could provide a suitable load for a low-impedance output circuit. But a speaker of higher impedance than required would not be utilised in this way, because of audio power lost in the resistor.

Audio Leads & Connectors

All low level audio input circuits should be of screened cable. These circuits include microphone leads, leads from tape and disc units or radio tuners, or associated with preamplifiers, mixers, and other equipment. The purpose of screening is to avoid introducing mains hum or interference into the following amplifier. Feedback from output to unscreened input circuits could also cause various forms of instability and similar troubles.

Single screened cable has an inner insulated conductor which is surrounded by braid or lapped wires, the whole being covered with PVC or other insulation. The inner conductor is used to carry audio signals, and the outer braid as the ground return for the microphone or other audio circuit. The braid, between units or elsewhere, is not used as a ground power conductor.

Single screened cable will be used for mono equipment and between single channel preamplifier and main amplifiers, and for similar purposes. Cables of normal length will have little effect on the performance, but the capacity loading introduced by long cables, especially in high impedance circuits, may have to be considered.

Twin or stereo cables can be used where two channels are required and are more tidy than two singles.

Screened cable with unscreened conductors enclosed in the overall covering is also available. These extra conductors may be employed for such purposes as switching on an amplifier by means of the push-switch fitted in a push-to-talk microphone. As some commercial equipment operates by closure of the PTT circuit to operate the amplifier, and others by opening of this circuit to operate it via a relay, equipment connecting details should be checked.

A special case arises with low power audio equipment, especially if operated from batteries. Due to lack of overall amplification or bass response, it may be possible to obtain satisfactory results with unscreened leads. This may allow as example the use of twin bell wire for a baby alarm or home intercom, or of twin flex between a tuner and its amplifier. This will depend on proximity to mains wiring, the input sensitivity or amplification of the equipment, and similar factors. Usually, screened cable would be fitted, but its use can be relaxed in some uncritical applications.

Loudspeakers can generally be fed by flat figure—8 2 amp flexible cable or any similar twin conductor. For normal output powers and speakers of 8 ohm and higher impedance, no appreciable loss of power is expected. Long cable to 2 ohm or similar units can introduce appreciable losses. These can be reduced by use of a stouter cable; by distribution of audio at a higher impedance; or shortened cables.

For single screened microphone and other audio leads, jack plugs are often used and are available in 3.5mm, 2.5mm, 0.25in and other sizes. The outer sleeve is for the braid connection, and inner or tip for the cable central conductor.

The plugs may be screened, giving maximum protection against hum etc. Or they may be insulated, so that the audio circuit is unshielded for a short distance.

The larger plugs are available for three circuits (2 sleeve plus tip). Jack sockets can have break or other contacts, operated by inserting the plug.

Other available plugs and sockets include those for loud-speaker use, 3, 4, 5 and more ways, flat pin and screened phono types, and lockable multi-way connectors. Various arrangements of these can be used for mono, stereo, interconnection of equipment, and other purposes, to suit the number of circuits and other details. Where home-built equipment is to be used with commercially made units or existing leads, care should be taken to obtain the correct fittings. As example, the 5-way plugs and sockets are used in both 180 degree and 240 degree types and these do not fit together. Various forms of ready-made interconnecting leads with plugs can be obtained, to avoid making these up.

Figure 28 shows 3-way and 5-way DIN sockets, at A and B. Either may be used for mono or stereo as follows:

3-way   Mono radio/recorder: 1 to recorder, 2 earth, 3 from recorder.
Stereo Amp: 1 LH channel in, 2 earth, 3 RH channel in.

5-way   Stereo radio/recorder: 1 LH channel to recorder, 2 earth, 3 LH channel from recorder, 4 RH channel to recorder, 5 RH channel from recorder.
Stereo recorder: 1 LH channel in, 2 earth, 3 LH channel out, 4 RH channel in, 5 RH channel out.

Output Jack Sockets

Jack plugs are convenient for loudspeaker and headphone connections with much equipment. The socket may be wired or arranged so that inserting a plug disconnects a permanently connected circuit. This is useful to silence a speaker when using a headset.

C, Figure 28, is a 3-circuit jack plug, with 1 for tip, 2 for ring, and 3 for sleeve contacts. D has tip contact 1 and sleeve 3. When a plug is inserted the circuit from 1 to 2 is broken.

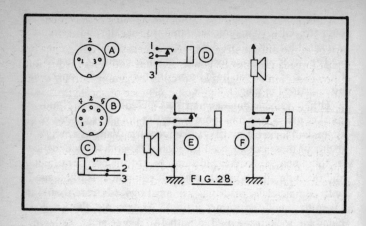

FIG.28.

With circuit E, the internal speaker is placed between the contact and ground. Inserting the plug breaks contact here, to silence the internal speaker. Audio signals are then available for the jack plug circuit only.

At F, the circuit is completed by means of the contact, so that a speaker permanently connected (as in a radio) operates when no plug is in the socket. Inserting a plug opens this circuit, and places the external load in series with the internal speaker.

Where the output circuit has to be returned to positive or the power line not grounded, insulated jack sockets can be used, or the metal type can be insulated from panel or case by means of bushes. The 2.5mm, 3.5mm and ¼in plugs and sockets are most popular, and actual designs vary considerably.

Care should be taken to avoid possible open circuits, or short-circuited output, which may damage the amplifiers.

Speakers & Phones

Loudspeakers are wound to provide a particular impedance. Typical speaker impedances are 2 ohm to 3 ohm, 4 ohm, 8 ohm, 15 ohm, 35 ohm and 64 ohm. Other impedances are encountered. For optimum possible results, the speaker used should be of the specified impedance. But for general purposes a near value, such as 16 ohm instead of 15 ohm, may be used.

A speaker of less than the minimum impedance specified for an IC or other amplifier should not be used, or peak current in the output stage may be too heavy. Often, somewhat higher impedances may be connected, but with some reduction in power output (though also a drop in maximum current drain). With some amplifiers, there may be a choice of speakers, depending on the power wanted, operating voltage, or other factors. For small (typically 250mW) transistor output circuits, the 64, 75 and 80 ohm units may be interchangeable.

A speaker will also have a peak power handling capacity. This may be 500mW (0.5W) or even less, for small units, such as are fitted to miniature receivers, and employed for similar purposes. Larger units will be for 1 watt, 2, 3, 4, 5, 10 watts, or greater powers. Clearly a speaker intended for, say, 1 watt, cannot be driven with the maximum output available from an amplifier delivering power beyond this level, or it is likely to receive mechanical damage. So the speaker unit should at least equal in power handling capacity the maximum output of the amplifier.

The speakers will also be available in various sizes, such as 2½in (64mm), 3 3/8in (86mm), 5in (127mm), 6½in (165mm), 8in (203mm) and other diameters. In general, the larger diameters will have greater power handling capacity. Thus a 64mm unit might be for 500mW, a 86mm unit for 1 watt, and a 203mm speaker for 10 watt outputs.

Various oval speakers are also available, such as 5 x 3in (127 x 76mm), 6 x 4in (156 x 105mm), 8 x 5in (203 x 127mm) and others. These can allow more compact cabinet assemblies.

The speaker should be operated in a cabinet, or at least with an adequate baffle board. A good, straightforward cabinet design can be one in which distances from the speaker to each edge are dissimilar, and are at least equal to the cone diameter. A baffle board is merely a stout, flat board, fairly large in size, with the speaker mounted behind an aperture. Various speaker cabinets and assemblies are also available.

Where two or more speakers are in use together, the cones should move in unison. Some units are marked to allow correct wiring. If not, apply a low DC voltage, and note which way the cone moves. Colour-code tags so that cones can be arranged to move together in the same direction with the same polarity. Impedances in series are approximately added. Thus two 8 ohm units in series would provide a 16 ohm load. Similarly, two 15 ohm units in parallel would result in a 7.5 ohm load (as for resistors in parallel).

A DC measurement of coil resistance is only a very rough guide to possible impedance, as DC resistance depends on wire gauge, etc. Impedance is normally several times DC resistance.

Headphones are also available in many types, and for géneral comfort and best listening a complete headset is recommended, not a single earpiece. The latter may be appropriate for an audio tracer, or portability.

For crystal diode receivers and other circuits where a high impedance load is required, a high impedance headset is necessary. This may be about 2,000 ohms, or 2k per phone. Fairly expensive phones of this type can be highly sensitive. They may be damaged by use in circuits which could pass a large direct current through the windings.

Stereo headphones or low-impedance phones may be about 8 ohm to 16 ohm. These cannot perform adequately where high impedance loads are required. Where audio power is limited by the type of equipment (e.g., diode radio) a matching transformer may be adopted to improve volume. Elsewhere, more than adequate power is likely to be available. Actual power necessary depends on the listener, phones and other factors, but may well be only a few milliwatts. Caution should be exercised when using phones on an amplifier intended for a speaker, as excess volume may jar the hearing, or damage the headset. A permanent resistor attenuator may be included in circuit for the phone outlet to avoid this.

Some general purpose earpieces may be of about 50 ohm to 200 ohm impedance, and are intended for use with receivers, etc. Crystal type earpieces are also used, and these provide no DC circuit, so must be capacitor coupled, or arranged so that a resistor allows transistor collector current, where required.

Where phones are often substituted for a speaker, reduced power with the latter can be arranged by using a higher impedance, and making up the amplifier load with a parallel resistor. A pre-set, or choice of fixed values, will allow any relative volume levels to be set up.

Switched Speaker/Phones

Where frequent change over from loudspeaker to headphones is required, it can be convenient to fit a 2-way switch for this purpose. This allows the phones to be permanently plugged in; the speaker may be internal or external to the equipment.

The circuit in Figure 29 provides a separate headphone volume control, which is set to give a suitable power level for the phones only, and has no effect with speaker reception. S is the 2-way switch, for speaker/phones selection. The phones are plugged in at socket P.

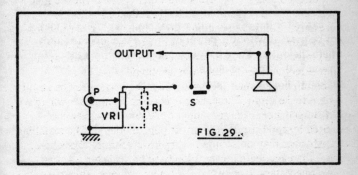

FIG. 29.

Where the phones and VR1 provide a suitable load, R1 is not required. For low impedance circuits and power up to 1w or so, VR1 can be a 10 ohm wire wound component, and 8 ohm phones may be used. If the phones are of high impedance, VR1 can be increased to 1k or more, and R1 will be added, of suitable resistance and wattage to provide a load for the amplifier. With a communications or other radio operating a 2 ohm or 3 ohm speaker, VR1 can be 10 ohm, and R1 about 3.3 ohm 1w, and almost any phones can be used.

For very high power outputs, such as when testing an amplifier, R1 must be present, of correct value and suitable wattage, and VR1 is merely an easy means of taking off lower level audio. With such equipment output must not be open circuit, or shorted, or below minimum specified load. Switch off before moving S from one position to the other.

Zobel Network

This consists of a capacitor and resistor in series, from the amplifier output point to negative line, or effectively in parallel with the loudspeaker. It would not be required where the output stage (individual transistors, or IC) is operating into a resistive load. However, with a loudspeaker, inductance can cause a voltage swing which can damage the output stage. This damage is, as would be expected, most likely when using near maximum voltage and output power. The network results in the total load being more nearly resistive, and it helps cancel or reduce the inductive element.

The network resembles a simple top-cut tone control, as the capacitor impedance falls when frequency rises. It may not be present with low power or low voltage operation, or where the output stage has adequate maximum voltage rating for use with a speaker alone. Some circuits may employ a capacitor alone in this position.

Miniature Audio Tracer

An audio tracer allows the signal present in audio equipment to be followed from its source, to locate a cause of failure. This is described more fully later.

The circuit in Figure 30 uses the TAA300 IC amplifier. This is of very small size, provides considerable gain, and operates well from a small 9v battery. (The maximum supply voltage for this IC is 10.5v). The presence of audio signals is located by touching the prod P on various circuit points. Clip C is attached to the ground line of the equipment, when necessáry. C1 is an isolating capacitor and 150v rating is easily adequate for ordinary transistor equipment.

Maximum gain is only needed for very low signal levels, and VR1 allows input to the IC to be kept down, as necessary for circuits where audio signals are already quite strong. C2 couples

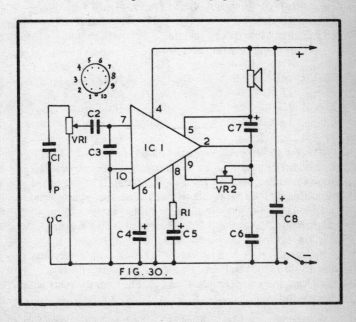

FIG. 30.

to the IC input at 7, and C3 is a by-pass capacitor.

C4 is for internal decoupling, R1 and C5 govern feedback and thus preset gain. The IC output stage feeds the speaker by C7, from 2. VR2 provides adjustable feedback to 9, to set the quiescent or no-signal current. (An internal circuit of this IC will be found in "Handbook of IC Audio Preamplifier & Power Amplifier Construction", BP35). The speaker is 8 ohm, and an earpiece can be used instead.

The IC has ten leads, numbered as shown, which can be arranged to fit the holes of the circuit board. Because of its very high gain, care is needed with the layout, to avoid instability. The by-pass capacitors are closely connected to the circuit points shown.

When the amplifier is first tested, place a meter in one battery supply lead, and adjust VR2 with a small screwdriver until the current drawn is about 7mA to 8mA, with no signal. This will peak up to 20mA to 40mA or so with a signal present, according to volume.

Components for Miniature Audio Tracer, Figure 30

R1	47 ohm	VR1	miniature 4.7k pot
VR2	miniature 22k horizontal pre-set potentiometer		with switch.
C1	47nF 150v	C2	10nF
C3	1nF	C4	100 μF
C5	22 μF	C6	47nF
C7	220 μF	C8	1000 μF
IC1	TAA300	Prod, clip, board, case, etc.	

If size is to be kept down and components fitted on the small board shown, small or miniature capacitors are needed. These are of low working voltage (excluding C1). The board is 2 x 5/8in (51 x 16mm). If wished, some extra space could be gained by following the same layout but using 0.15in matrix board, instead of 0.1in. The board is 20 x 6 holes, with foils horizontal in Figure 30B.

For clarity, only foils necessary for circuit continuity are shown, and as broken lines. Elsewhere, make foil breaks, taking care these are complete, and that no contact arises with adjacent foils.

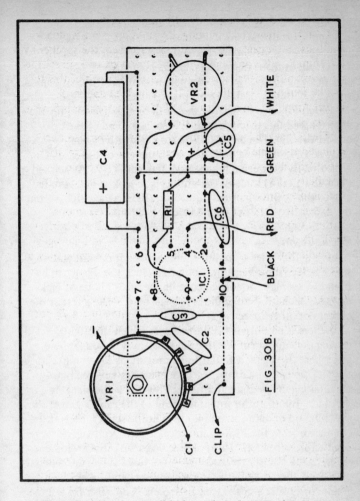

FIG. 30B.

VR1 is fitted with a small bolt, and projects so that it can extend through a slot in the case. C4 lies over the board. IC1 is not included in Figure 30B for clarity. Arrange its leads to fit the numbered holes as shown, and solder underneath in the usual way. Note the wire from negative line to the foil which supports C4 negative; and also that from 9 to VR2.

Thin colour coded leads are soldered on, red from 4, and

65

white from 5. It is necessary to accommodate C7 and C8 on the underside of the board. Solder C7 from IC5 foil to IC2 foil, negative at hole marked green, and C8 from IC4 foil to 1—10 foil, bringing negative up at the hole marked 'black'. It is possible to arrange the components so that the board and a small 9v battery will fit a small case. Take a flexible lead about 1ft (300mm) or so long from the earth or negative line, for the clip. Thread this through a small hole in the end of the case, and fit the clip. The prod is made from a length of 6ba screwed rod, or a long bolt, locked to the end of the case. C1 goes directly between a tag secured here and VR1. Attach red (4) and white (5) leads to the output jack socket, and take red also to the positive battery connector. Battery negative is from the switch at VR1. Set VR2 as explained earlier.

Circuit Testing

Assuming that a set of audio equipment is not operating, test step by step from the earliest point at which the signal can be found. This may for convenience be the microphone or pick-up input socket. If no audio is present here, make a test at the pick-up or other source of AF itself.

If there is no output from the device which should be driving the equipment, clearly the fault must be sought here. But where the signal is found to be present, as for example at the pick-up end of a cable, tests are made systematically from here, taking in one item at a time. Thus the audio signal should be found at the equipment end of the cable, then at the jack plug tip or appropriate pin, then at the socket, then at the conductor from the socket, and then at the circuit foil or conductor, and so on. If the signal ceases, an interruption has arisen in the last item introduced — fractured cable, disconnected plug, lack of contact between plug and socket, broken conductor, broken board foil, and so on. Look also for a short to ground.

In practice, tests are readily speeded up. As example, if the signal is present at the circuit board input point, this clears all earlier items, so detailed tests are unnecessary. But it is by step by step tests that an actual break in the audio circuit can be localised. Faulty cables, joints, plug contacts and switch contacts will be included, and also items such as foils with hair-line breaks, capacitors with an end lead adrift, and so on.

As a stage is introduced so that audio level rises, turn down gain by VR1. If the signal is present at the base or input of a transistor amplifier, but not at its collector or output, then the stage is suspected. A meter test of associated resistors should show where this fault lies. Voltage tests can also show if the expected collector and other voltages are present. If not, meter tests will show if the transistor is at fault, or a resistor or shorted capacitor, or defect in the power supply here.

In general, some experiment and practice will show what to expect, and how tests are carried through.

The audio tracer should not be used on any valve equipment or mains equipment where high voltages will be present.

Pen Generator

This pen sized multivibrator produces an audio output which can be used to locate faults in amplifiers, interconnecting leads, and other items. Figure 31 shows the circuit, intended to run from a single 1.5v dry cell. Each transistor drives the other, and the values are chosen to give a suitable output. This is taken from the collector of Tr2, via C3 and R5. A miniature spring loaded push is used for on-off, located in the positive lead.

A circuit of this kind will operate with a wide range of values and transistors, but by using miniature ceramic disc 10nF capacitors size is kept down. Miniature 1/8th watt or similar resistors are also adequate.

Components for Pen Generator Figure 31

R1, R4, R5	2.2k	R2, R3	47k
C1, C2, C3	10nF	Tr1, Tr2	2N3706

Figure 31 also shows assembly, which is without any kind of circuit board or mounting for the components. Turn one transistor so that emitters E face each other, and solder a wire between them. R1 and R2 are then arranged above Tr1 and soldered to collector (centre lead) and base. Solder R4 to collector of Tr2 and R3 to base, join them near R3, and run on a lead to the junction of R1/R2. From here, a lead will go to the push switch, and from switch to battery positive. Connect

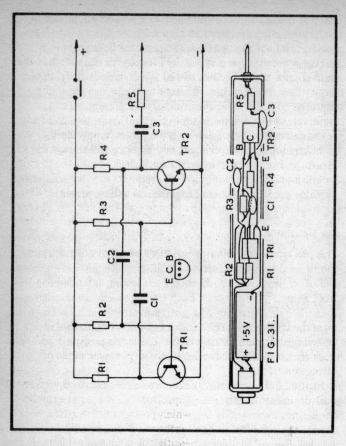

FIG. 31.

C1 from Tr1 collector to Tr2 base, and C2 from Tr1 base to Tr2 collector. C3 and R5 are also added.

It is best to stagger joints and components somewhat, and to put small diameter sleeving right up to the bodies of resistors and capacitors. C2 can lie over R4, and C3 over Tr2.

The prod is a long 8ba screw, filed to a point, and the whole assembly is arranged so that it will slide down into the container. A small nut then holds the prod in place. If the case is metal, the prod must be insulated by washers, and the assembly can be rolled in a tube of stout paper before sliding it into place. Various household containers, tablet holders and similar items may be pressed into service, or a case made from paxolin or other tube, or devised from a fairly large pen.

To use the generator, apply the prod to various points in the audio circuit, and press the switch. Work backwards from the output stage, if the source of a break is to be located. Otherwise the signal may be applied stage by stage, when its amplified tone should be heard in the speaker.

With an audio tracer (Figure 30) tests are made step by step from the source of the audio signal. With a generator used for tests, these proceed step by step backwards through the circuit from the output stage.

Where the signal is too strong, but the point tested is after the volume control, the easiest way to reduce volume is to take a resistor and twist it to the prod, so that it is in series with R5. Values up to 1 megohm or so may be used in this way, depending on the equipment sensitivity and input impedance of the point tested.

Level Meters

An audio level meter may be used for obtaining a suitable recording level, noting the level of signals on the public address or other circuit, or for balancing stereo outputs and similar purposes.

Figure 32 shows a mono circuit at A. Output is taken from a driver stage to the isolating capacitor C1. R1 supplies audio frequencies to the diode D1, which provides rectification to operate the meter M1. C2 smooths out peaks, so that M1 indicates average loudness. Sensitivity may be adjusted by R2, R1, or the choice of M1. If wished, R2 can be pre-set, to allow maximum reading on M1 to correspond to maximum audio level permitted.

The circuit at B is for stereo, and uses a meter with central zero. It is connected so that when LH channel signals are stronger, the pointer moves to the left, movement to the right being obtained when RH signals are stronger. D2 and D3 are matched diodes, and R3/R4 and C3/C4 are also equal. VR1 allows adjustment of sensitivity. If this is too great, a small lack of balance will drive the meter fully one way. This depends

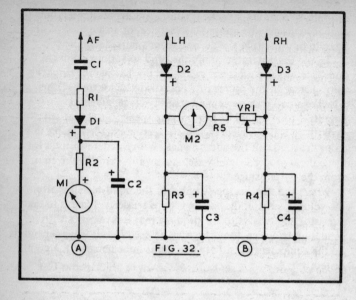

FIG. 32.

on power applied, and impedance of the loudspeakers or output circuits from which the LH and RH channel connections are taken.

Either of these circuits can operate satisfactorily with quite a wide range of meters, provided resistor and capacitor values are modified to suit.

Components for Level Meters, Figure 32

R1	4.7k	R2	56k
C1, C2	6.4 μF	D1	OA91, etc.
M1	100 μA level meter	C3, C4	100 μF
R3, R4	4.7k	VR1	22k pre-set
R5	4.7k	M2	500 μA or 1mA
D2, D3	OA91, etc.		centre-zero

Sine Wave Source

Audio frequency oscillators as used for circuit testing and similar purposes generally produce unsymmetrical, spiky waveforms rich in harmonics. They are not suitable where an

70

amplifier is to be tested with sine wave input, for a check of maximum power output in these conditions. For this purpose, an oscillator producing a sine wave output is necessary. For simplicity, this can work on a single frequency.

The circuit in Figure 33 requires only two transistors, and has a very good output. It is for 9v. Frequency can be modified by changing the values of C1 and C2, and R1 and R2. As C1 equals C2 in value, and R1 equals R2, only C1 and R1 need be considered. The frequency is then approximately:

$$\frac{1}{6.28 \times C1 \times R1}$$

As example, assume 0.02 μF with 4.7k. 6.28 x 0.02 x 4700 = 590.32. Replacing 1 by 1,000,000 (because capacitance was in micro-farads) gives 1,000,000/590.32 = 1594Hz (nearly). Frequency is not exact due to loading by other parts of the circuit, but this can be used as a guide for other frequencies. (A variable sine wave generator is shown in "Electronic Test

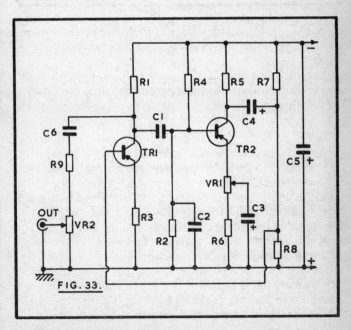

FIG. 33.

71

Equipment Construction", BP75).

R1 is also the collector load of Tr1. R2 and R4 are a divider for the base of Tr2. R5 is collector load for Tr2, with feedback to Tr1 base by C4, and R7 and R8 for base divider.

Output is taken from Tr1 collector by C6 and R9, to a simple attenuator VR2. Output frequency is almost wholly independent of output.

A scope will generally be used to observe the output waveform of the amplifier being tested, and the output from VR2 can be taken to this, and VR1 can be set to suit supply voltage and transistors, for the best sine wave. VR2 can then be calibrated by means of the scope for peak output, though this will naturally be lower with a lower impedance load attached here. Output level is small.

Other transistors and values may be used. As mentioned, the base bias conditions for Tr1 depend largely on R7/R8, and for Tr2 largely on R2/R4, so may be adjusted to suit other types.

Components for Sine Wave Source, Figure 33

R1, R2, R5	4.7k	R3	3.3k
R4	27k	R6	1k
R7	39k	R8	10k
R9	22k	VR1	1k pre-set
VR2	100k pot	C1, C2	0.02 μF
C3	8 μF	C4	1 μF
C5	100 μF	C6	0.1 μF
Tr1, Tr2 OC70		Tagboard, case, etc.	

As a substitute for the transistors listed, 2N3702s may be used. Figure 33B shows components assembled on a tabgoard. The board is mounted on the cover of an alloy box, with spacers or nuts to give a little clearance. Take a lead from the tag to be employed for C5 positive to a tag secured by one of these bolts, to ground the case. Similarly earth VR2 to the panel at the output socket. A box about 4 x 3 x 1½in (102 x 76 x 38mm) will also take a battery.

VR1 is a vertical preset, soldered to tags as shown, and set with a screwdriver as explained. C1 and C2 may be put on last, in such a way that they can easily be changed if the frequency is to be altered. A 2.5mm or 3.5mm jack socket will take a

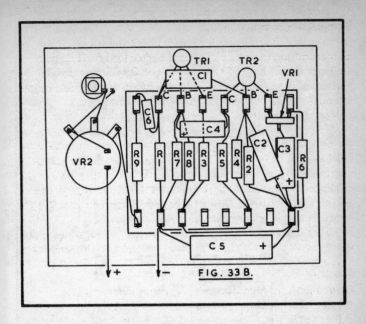

FIG. 33 B.

plug and screened lead to supply an amplifier to be tested. Screened assembly in this way will help avoid picking up hum and introducing this into the equipment.

Dummy Audio Load

When testing an audio amplifier, a dummy load to replace the loudspeaker is helpful. This will provide various loads, and also avoid the powerful audio resulting from the use of a speaker.

Figure 34 shows a suitable method, using four 8 ohm 10 watt resistors. Other arrangements and values can be used, or a resistor for one load only, where only this is required. Switching is scarcely worthwhile. Two terminal strips will allow the resistors to be connected in various combinations.

At A one resistor provides for 8 ohm 10w, while at B two in series provide a 16 ohm load able to take 20w. C is 24 ohm 30w. At E, two in parallel provide 4 ohm 20w. F places 8 ohm and 4 ohm in series for 12 ohm, 15w. G is 32 ohm

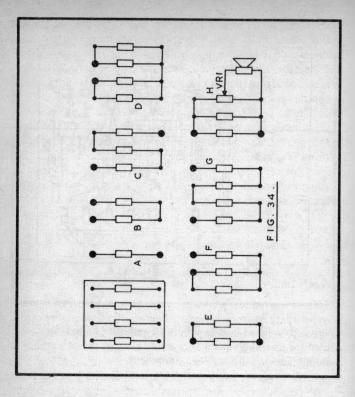

FIG. 34.

40w, and D 8 ohm 40w.

Resistor wattages are generally continuous ratings. Where the tests will only be for a short time, some over-running can be allowed. For a smaller load unit, 8.2 ohm 2w resistors can be used instead.

At H, potentiometer VR1 allows a small part of the audio signal to be taken, at much reduced volume, for monitoring. Here, the speaker can be a small 15 ohm to 75 ohm unit, and VR1 can be 2k, wire-wound. The change in load from VR1 and the speaker is negligible at low impedances. VR1 must be set nearly at minimum, with all but small amplifiers, or the speaker will be damaged.

Output power ratings are commonly expressed as continuous power, or music power. A continuous power rating is one the

74

amplifier should be able to deliver, with sinewave input, for at least 30 seconds. Music power represents almost instantaneous values, where power supply voltage has not had time to drop. The latter rating allows a higher figure. Ratings may also be specified at a particular distortion level, or when clipping commences.

The onset of peak clipping is best observed with a sine-wave input, dummy load, and oscilloscope. The voltage across the load can also be found by this means, and power calculated from this. Many testmeters are also satisfactory at audio frequency (reference should be made to the maker's information). A meter test will then also show the voltage developed across the output load.

Wattage is found by squaring the voltage and dividing by the load resistance. As example, assume 10v found across 8 ohm. $V^2/R = 10 \times 10/8 = 100/8 = 12.5w$.

Audio Limiter

This circuit reduces gain with a strong signal input, to avoid overloading an amplifier or modulator. Similar circuits may also be used for recording, to reduce level when gain is too high for the microphone output.

Audio input is at A, Figure 35. With no signal, or low volume, base bias conditions for Tr1 depend on R1, and R2 with R5. R3 is the collector load, and C2 couples signals into the main amplifier, by means of socket B.

Point C receives audio from the loudspeaker circuit, or from elsewhere in the amplifier as described later. Part of this audio voltage is tapped off by the potentiometer VR1, and is rectified by D1, producing a negative voltage across C4. This reaches the junction of R2 and R5 from R6, and moves Tr1 base negative, reducing gain.

C3, R6 and C4 prevent feedback at audio frequencies, which would cause instability. C3 and C4 cannot be too large in value, or there is too great a time lag in restoring gain after high volume. Some delay is necessary, so that response does not arise to the ordinary gap between words, and similar brief intervals.

Sufficient audio power should be available at C to produce about 1v across R5, with VR1 at about half position.

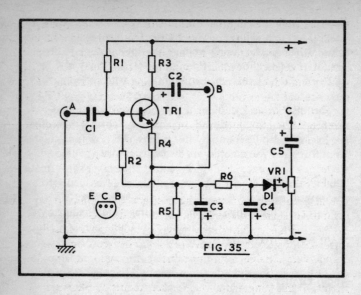

FIG. 35.

For best results, it is necessary to adjust the signal level at A, amplifier gain, and VR1 setting. Very high inputs at A will overload Tr1. The main amplifier must have enough gain and output to produce the control voltage mentioned. R4 helps to avoid distortion in Tr1, but cannot compensate for all conditions.

Characteristics of the circuit can be modified by altering the resistor values, especially R1, and R2 or R5. Reducing R5 (or C3 and C4) also reduces the delay.

Components for Audio Limited, Figure 35

R1	100k	R2	68k
R3	10k	R4	150 ohm
R5	22k	R6	2.2k
VR1	2k pot	C1	0.33 μF
C2	1 μF	C3	22 μF
C4	47 μF	C5	33 μF
Tr1	2N3706, etc.	D1	OA90, etc.

Layout should keep C5 and components and circuits here away from C1 and associated items, including C2. Actual stray feedback from the amplifier output circuit at C to its input at B will result in howling and instability. Use a shielded lead at B, and direct connection to the negative line of the amplifier for ground, if needed. Feedback round the loop C5, D1, R6, R2, via Tr1 and C2, can be checked by turning VR1 to zero. A very slow rise and fall in volume can be caused by advancing VR1 too far, so that C3/C4 charge, cutting off signals, then discharge through R5/R6, when the sequence is repeated. A 4.5v supply is suitable.

Light Modulator

This automatically provides lighting effects to accompany tape, radio or vocal and other entertainment. In disco presentations or stage lighting coloured spotlamps or other lights are used, with control circuits responsive to a range of frequencies. Three channels are suitable, with three differently coloured lamps, or sets of lamps. One colour is controlled by the high frequency circuit, so this lamp lights when higher frequency tones are strongly present. The second colour is produced by middle frequencies, and the third by low frequency tones. There is thus a constantly changing display, depending on the beat, frequency and power of the musical elements.

Simple circuits cannot provide a sharp cut-off from one range of frequencies to another, and such an effect is not really required. Operation can then be controlled by capacitors, whose reactance falls as frequency rises.

Figure 36 shows the circuit for three lamps (or sets of lamps). Transformer T1 receives audio signals from the amplifier loudspeaker circuit, and also isolates the light modulator from the amplifier. Higher audio frequencies pass C1 and VR1, and reach gate G of the silicon controlled rectifier SCR1. When the gate G is driven sufficiently positive relative to the cathode K, the SCR conducts from cathode K to anode A, passing current through the HF lamp L1.

As the circuit is operating from AC, the SCR goes out of conduction each time the anode is negative. Resistor R1 is to prevent too ready triggering of the SCR. As a result, illumination of L1 closely follows the audio signal present at

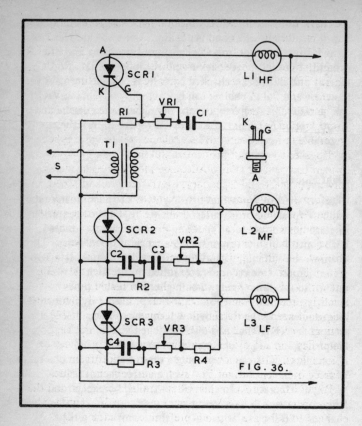

FIG. 36.

the SCR gate.

Response to middle and lower frequencies can be reduced by fitting a smaller capacitance at C1. Sensitivity of the response of SCR1 is adjusted by VR1. Generally, only a very low voltage is needed at the gate, but this varies with different SCRs. Sensitivity increases at VR1 is reduced in value. If operation is too sensitive with all of VR1 is circuit, R1 can be reduced in value.

SCR2 controls the medium frequency lamp L2 in the same way, except that C2 tends to suppress response to high frequencies, and C3 blocks low frequencies. VR2 is set so that L2 only responds to quite strong middle frequencies. Should the characteristics of the SCR make it necessary, sensitivity can be changed as described for SCR1.

SCR3 similarly controls the low frequency lamp L3, and C4 makes this circuit most responsive to LF. R4 avoids shunting HF out of the drive line to SCR1 and SCR2 by setting VR3 to zero.

Operation is possible with relatively low audio power (under 1 watt amplifiers) if the SCRs are of sensitive type. It is preferable to have greater drive available. Mains valve type loudspeaker coupling transformers and small mains transformers can be used at T1. Adequate insulation is needed between primary and secondary, for the reason mentioned. A transformer with a step-up ratio of about 10:1 can be used at T1, and is obtained with a 240v/24v mains transformer, with 24v winding employed as primary. Where the audio output voltage is too high, a resistor can be placed in series with T1 primary. For an amplifier giving modest power and using a 2 ohm or 3 ohm speaker, a step-up ratio will be essential at T1. But with a 15 ohm speaker and medium or higher power amplifier, the ratio can be much lower, or even 1:1. The most important need is to obtain enough drive to allow suitable settings for VR1, VR2 and VR3, so that HF, MF and LF lamps flash on and off suitably when music is reproduced at normal level. There is a very large range of adjustment possible in the circuit, by T1, resistor and capacitor values.

Power from the AC mains will be at 50Hz or 60Hz, and the lamps operate with half-wave power in Figure 36. This can be changed to full-wave, which is preferable, by adding the rectifiers in Figure 37.

The rectifiers have to be rated for the maximum total current of the lamps. With 1A rectifiers, lamps are limited to about 240w in all — say 3 x 75w (225w). For larger loads, appropriately larger rectifiers are needed. Silicon diodes with 1k PIV rating are suitable. Output from the rectifiers is at 100Hz (or 120Hz) with the SCRs able to fall out of conduction at the zero following each half-cycle. Thus smoothing must not be added.

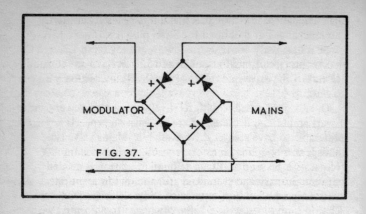

MODULATOR   MAINS

FIG. 37.

Components for Light Modulator, Figure 36

R1, R2, R3	8.2k	R4	5.6k
VR1, VR2, VR3	22k linear pots.	C1	47nF
		C3	68nF
C2	33nF	SCR1, 2, 3	500v 1A
C4	0.47 μF	T1	See Text
L1, L2, L3	60w 240v		

Construction can best place T1, SCRs and other items in a grounded metal case, having VR1, VR2 and VR3 on the front, and fitted with numbered dials. Sockets for mains type plugs will take leads for L1, L2 and L3. It is considered that lamps such as L1, L2 and L3 should be taken to the Neutral main, for maximum safety when they may be changed. This places T1 at the Live side of the circuit, so that its insulation must be adequate. Circuits will be found with lamps such as those L1, L2 and L3 at the Live side of the circuit, and this allows T1 to be at the Neutral (or low potential relative to earth) side of the mains. In all cases mains circuits must of course be properly wired, with mains type fittings properly used. This includes earthing of metal reflectors or lamp fittings, by 3-core cords, taken to the modulator. In no circumstance should any of the proper safety precautions be omitted. Such precautions are designed to make equipment safe to handle, and to assure that it remains safe even under fault conditions. Power for the modulator is drawn by a 3-core cord, to provide proper earthing, and a low-rating fuse should be present in the L conductor — this will be in the 3-pin plug itself, with 13A type plugs.

Suppressor capacitors can be added from cathode to anode at each SCR, and across the mains input leads. These may be 0.1 μF to 0.22 μF, 1kV, or as available for vacuum cleaners etc.

CW Filter

This is an audio frequency filter to use when receiving CW Morse. Filters of this type are found in expensive communications receivers, and are intended to favour a narrow band of audio frequencies. When receiving CW, the beat frequency oscillator of the receiver is so adjusted that the audible beat note falls in the filter pass-band. As a result, this audio tone (the wanted signal) is passed, while interfering signals on other frequencies are attenuated. The general effect is that of making the wanted CW signal stand out above noise and unwanted signals.

In Figure 38 Tr1 is a source follower operating into the filter. Input to R1 can be from the detector or other low-level audio section of the receiver. It is also possible to take audio from the speaker circuit, where this is isolated by a transformer. In this case, an audio load such as a 3.3 ohm 1 watt resistor should be connected to replace the speaker, where a 2/3 ohm unit is disconnected.

As the filter is not requied for speech reception, a 2-way 2-pole switch introduces R5 instead. The unit then substitutes for the audio amplifier of the receiver, without disconnection and reconnection being required. In either case audio passes from R7 and C6 to the audio gain or volume control VR1, and to input 8 of the audio IC amplifier. This particular IC has been dealt with in detail elsewhere, and output is to a speaker S, 8 ohm to 16 ohm impedance. Operation can be from a 9v battery, or 12v supply.

The filter elements consist primarily of L1 with C3 and L2 with C5, coupled by C4, and operating with input load of R3 and R4, and output load of R6, approximately 2.7k in each case. C3, C4 and C5 should be close values (2 per-cent or 5 per-cent preferred) and there is some adjustment by means of

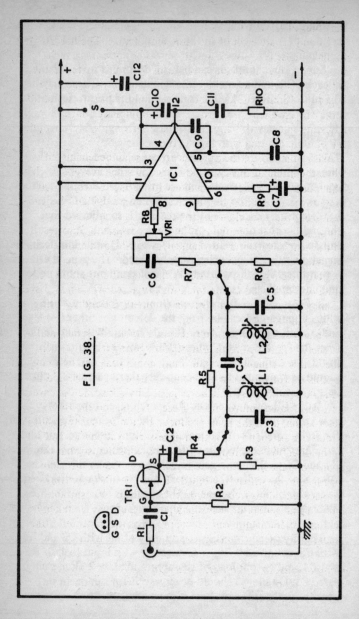

FIG. 38.

82

the cores of L1 and L2.

L1 and L2 are each of the same inductance. The neatest way to make these is to use "Siferrit" or other pot cores which provide a known inductance per turn. With this material, the N28 type is suitable for this and higher audio frequencies. Using the 18mm cores with single section bobbins to suit, 500 turns of 42swg wire are used. Each bobbin has a central adjusting screw with flange. The material completely surrounds the bobbin, as usual with high-Q type coils.

With other cores, the number of turns can be calculated when the inductance value is known, and some makers list this. The inductance values are smaller with smaller cores, so that more turns are needed, and these can become difficult because extremely fine wire then has to be used. Unknown or ex-equipment cores might be usable, by experiment. Some adjustment to inductance is helpful, as this allows compensation for hand-winding, or exact capacitor values.

Components for such an audio filter may be found in an otherwise discarded communications type receiver, and C3 and C5 may be preset or compression trimmers, L1 and L2 being of fixed inductance.

To adjust L1 and L2, first tune in a stable CW signal, and set the BFO control for about 800Hz. Swing it a little each side of this frequency, to find if any audio peak can be found. If so, this is probably from resonance in L1 or L2. It should be possible to shift the frequency slightly, by adjusting the core of L1 or L2, and to move one of these circuits, and the BFO heterodyne, until the peak produced by the second resonant circuit can be found. It is then necessary to adjust L1 and L2 in the direction which brings the peaks together, so that there is only one much sharper audio resonance. Once this is done, no further adjustment is needed. In use, the BFO is always set to place the audio frequency in this position. If a suitable audio signal generator is available, its output may be taken to R1, and its frequency can be swept across the expected filter resonant frequency, to find and adjust L1 and L2.

Components for CW Filter, Figure 38

| R1 | 39 ohm | R2 | 1 megohm |
| R3 | 680 ohm | R4 | 2.2k |

R5	10k	R6, R7	2.7k
R8	4.7k	R9	47 ohm
R10	1 ohm	VR1	100k log pot
C1	10nF	C2	6.4 μF
C3, C5	0.34 μF	C4	68nF
C6	2.2 μF	C7	100 μF
C8	2700pF	C9	330pF
C10	1000 μF	C11	0.1 μF
C12	1000 μF	Tr1	MPF103/2N5457, etc.
IC1	TBA800	L1, L2	88mH

This unit has been constructed on plain 0.15in board, to fit a case approximately 6 x 4 x 2½in (152 x 102 x 64mm) and this is probably most suitable, as it allows point to point wiring below. The 2-way switch, VR1 and on-off switch are fitted to the panel. A screened lead carries audio to the input socket.

Other audio amplifiers could be placed after the filter, depending on the amplification and power required, and whether output is for speaker or headphones.

VOX Unit

A voice operated or sound operated relay finds application in various projects. It is frequently used in transceiver circuits, so that speaking automatically switches the equipment to the transmit condition. A VOX unit can be arranged to perform this function with some home-built or ready manufactured transmitters without much difficulty.

In the home, such a device is useful to provide an automatic extension for a telephone or doorbell. Ringing will then actuate the relay, which can operate a bell or light in a distant room, or where it may be seen or heard when watching TV or otherwise engaged in household activities. Such an arrangement, sound operated, needs no actual connection to the telephone or doorbell.

Figure 39 is the circuit, and it is intended to use a small 2½in to 3½in (60—90mm) speaker of about 70 to 80 ohm impedance as the pick-up unit or microphone. The VOX will operate from other microphones, but sensitivity may be

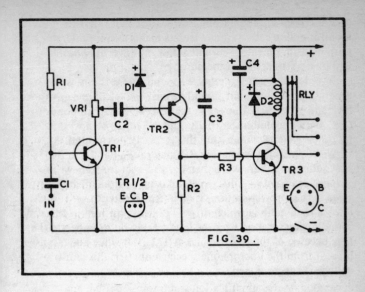

FIG. 39.

reduced. It is also in order to take low-level audio from an
amplifier stage to C1, when using the VOX in conjunction
with a modulator or other equipment.

Tr1 is an audio amplifier, with base current from R1, and
VR1 as the collector load. This allows sensitivity to be
adjusted, and audio passes from C2 to diode D1 and the base of
the PNP transistor Tr2. Here, rectification of audio signals
drives Tr2 base negative, so that collector current through R2
increases, moving R3 and the base of Tr3 positive. Capacitor
C3 is to provide delay so that the relay does not immediately
drop out, between words.

When Tr3 base moves positive, collector current increases,
and the relay is operated. Closure of these contacts can switch
on (or off) any external circuit. With a 100 ohm relay and 9v
supply, the current rises to about 50mA to 75mA. A 12v
supply can be used, with a slight increase in current here. In
general, a relay of about 100 to 250 ohms, and operating with
25mA to 50mA or so, will be most suitable. With a relay of
higher resistance, current will be very low, though this is not
important if the relay is sufficiently sensitive to operate. A
low resistance relay cannot be used, however.

85

For continuous operation, as when the unit is left to monitor phone calls, running from a mains unit is preferable. With no sound present, current is low, however, and battery working is feasible for some purposes.

In order to select the required sound, and not noises in general, the pick-up unit should be near the telephone or other bell, and VR1 should be set so that the VOX only responds to this. With maximum sensitivity, the relay may be operated by other, general sounds, and this is clearly not wanted.

With transceiver operation, C1 may take audio from the first audio amplifier. VR1 then has to be set for somewhat reduced sensitivity. Anti-trip audio is taken from an audio stage in the receiver section, via a potentiometer to set the level, and to a diode which drives Tr2 base positive. In this way sounds being received over the loudspeaker do not operate the trip, because of the positive bias at Tr2. But when audio is present from the microphone speech amplifier, this anti-trip voltage is not produced.

Components for VOX Unit, Figure 39

R1	1.8 megohm	R2	4.7k
R3	1k	VR1	5k pot
C1	0.1 μF	C2	0.22 μF
C3	30 μF	C4	1000 μF
Tr1	2N3706	Tr2	2N3702
Tr2	2N3503	D1	OA90, etc
D2	1N4002	RLY	100–150 ohm, 50mA

Construction on a tagboard is shown in Figure 39B. For a separate unit, a small metal case will help screen Tr1 base circuit against pick-up of hum or interference which may trigger the relay. The miniature speaker can be accommodated in the case, so that this can be placed near the telephone or other bell. If the speaker (or microphone) is at a little distance, it may be necessary to use screened lead here — this depends on the lead length, and proximity of mains wiring. Keep relay leads away from input leads, to avoid feedback which may result in the circuit being unstable.

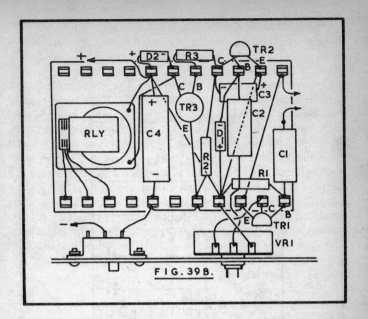

FIG.39B.

Tuner for Amplifiers

This tuner will provide reception over the range approximately
1600–550kHz medium wave. It does not have the sensitivity
and selectivity of a superhet tuner, but is adequate for the
more powerful stations, and gives very good quality, so is an easy
means of obtaining radio programmes with an amplifier.

Tr1, Figure 40, is a dual-gate FET, with gain controlled by
VR1. VR1 also reduces signal input at coupling winding L1
when its wiper is towards the minimum gain setting. R1 and R2
provide a fixed potential for Gate 2. Output from Drain D is
to the coupling winding L3, taken to positive.

L2 and L4 tune together, by the ganged capacitor VC1/VC2.
This component has integral trimmers. If not, an external
trimmer of about 50pF may be connected in parallel with each
section. Diode D1 is tapped down L4 to reduce damping on
this circuit. Audio output is from capacitor C5.

Medium wave coils with coupling windings can be used, and
are available from several suppliers. Figure 40 shows winding

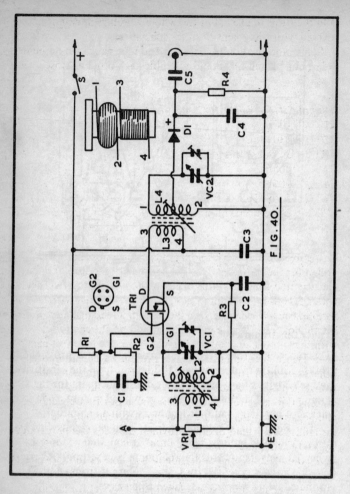

FIG. 40.

details for home-made coils, using 7mm formers with adjustable cores, and 34swg enamelled wire. Starting at 1, wind 115 turns in a pile occupying 8mm or 5/16th in, finishing at 2. Leave a very small space, and beginning at 3, wind on thirty turns side by side, finishing at 4. As far as possible wind the coils in exactly the same way, but make the tapping for D1 negative at 60 turns from 2 on L4. Traces of adhesive will hold the turns in place, but the whole windings must not be covered with wax, paint or other substances.

Some modification to diameter and wire gauge would be in order, but L2 and L4 should resemble each other as closely as possible.

Components for Tuner for Amplifiers, Figure 40

R1	100k	R2	68k
R3	330 ohm	R4	27k
VR1	5k pot with switch	C1	10nF
C2	20nF	C3	0.1 μF
C4	100pF	C5	0.47 μF
VC1/2	2 x 365pF or similar	D1	OA90, etc.
	ganged capacitor	Panel, case, knobs, etc.	
Tr1	40673	L1–L4	See Text

Figure 40B shows a wired layout, using a paxolin board drilled for the purpose. This is a convenient method of construction for small units, using plain, non-perforated sheet about 1/16th in or 1½mm thick, or materials other than paxolin, such as perspex, or a piece from a rectangular plastic box, etc. Brittle materials should be cut carefully, with sharp tools, or they may crack. Mark the holes on paper from Figure 40B, and use this as a guide for a 1/16th in or other very small drill. The board is held by a bracket made from scrap metal, which is in turn secured by the bolts holding the capacitor to the panel. Capacitor frame, panel, and negative (earth) line are all connected together. No instability was found to arise provided the coils were separated by VC1/2 and quite far apart.

Figure 40 shows the underside of Tr1, and note that Gate 1 and Gate 2 must not be interchanged. VR1 and switch S are under the board, and also a 3.5mm panel socket for audio output, from C5.

Initially place the cores so that they are about half way in L1/L2, and L3/L4. Attach an aerial to A, and earth to E. A small 9v battery can be used for the supply. Tune in a signal with VC1/2 nearly open, and adjust the trimmers for best volume. Then find a transmission with VC1/2 nearly closed, and adjust the cores for maximum volume. Repeat a few times.

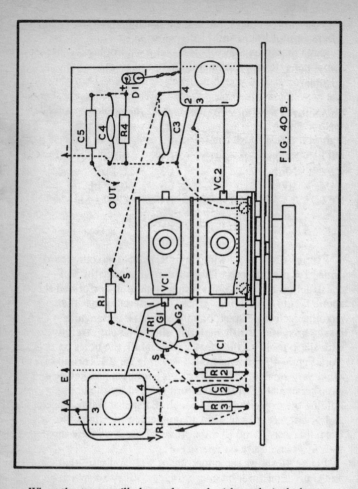

FIG. 40 B.

When the tuner will always be used with a relatively low gain amplifier, a single transistor audio stage can be fitted after C5, to provide a boosted output. The earth may be omitted if there is effective earthing through the amplifier equipment. The aerial will considerably influence results. If it is very long, place a 100pF or other preset capacitor between the lead-in and terminal A.

Please note overleaf is a list of other titles that are available in our range of Radio and Electronics Books.

These should be available from all good Booksellers, Radio Component Dealers and Mail Order Companies.

However, should you experience difficulty in obtaining any title in your area, then please write directly to the publisher enclosing payment to cover the cost of the book plus adequate postage.

If you would like a catalogue of our complete range of Radio and Electronics Books, then please send a Stamped Addressed Envelope to:—

BERNARD BABANI (publishing) LTD
THE GRAMPIANS
SHEPHERDS BUSH ROAD
LONDON W6 7NF
ENGLAND